New Day

God's Revelation to a Hidden Prophetic Voice

Gregory A. Gibson

FOREFRONT

Contact us at:

forefrontcanada@gmail.com

ISBN: 978-1-77354-284-3

Dedication

To all the faithful, hidden prophetic voices that our gracious Heavenly Father has placed throughout the earth for such a time as this. May our collective voice break through the wilderness and point anyone and everyone toward the coming of our great King and His unshakeable Kingdom!

Contents

Revelation

1. God's disclosure of Himself and His will to His creatures.
2. An instance of such communication or disclosure.
3. Something thus communicated or disclosed.
4. Something that contains such disclosure.

Preface

Adventure is a word that is rarely used in relation to Christianity. I am here to tell you that it should be. There is no greater adventure than sitting with the God of the universe. Conversations with our Creator are far from boring and seldom unnoteworthy.

The entirety of this book consists of such meetings. They have been recorded—in most part—as they transpired onto the pages of my daily journals as I met with the LORD each day, over the past year or so. You may notice that in each chapter, a theme is developed and as the entries progress, become deeper, richer and more developed than ones given previously. Of course, in His infinite wisdom, the LORD spoke to one theme one day and another the next, weaving together messages given days apart.

And if you are led to engage these pages, you will find that our LORD deeply cares for you and the entire population of the earth. For contained within the pages of this book are God's thoughts on the Covid-19 virus, the fear and chaos that came with the pandemic, and His response to such a catastrophic interruption to the world. From its first pages it will become evident that while He did not cause the disruption, the LORD not only *knew* all that was going on behind the scenes, but what lay ahead in a glorious future as well!

Clearly, our sovereign, omnipotent God was not surprised by anything that transpired over the months of lockdowns and protocols that plagued the globe. When nothing seemed dependable, normal or trustworthy, Jesus provided a consistent answer. He became a shelter, a solid place of support and guidance to anyone willing to seek Him out in this way.

It is hoped that this book will not only serve as a testimony to the faithfulness of our God to meet regularly and abundantly with anyone willing to seek Him earnestly, but also to the authenticity of the great love that our heavenly Father has for all of mankind. His desire is that all would seek and see Him for who He is: The Savior of the World!

So, I invite you to step into these pages and give His words a chance to minister to your soul. The planet has been through one of the most traumatic periods in all of its existence. Not one person has escaped its harsh elements and challenging seasons. We are a populace in need of healing. Allow Jesus to bring direction, alignment and—most importantly—His truth to you.

A New Day has dawned, and a new era is upon us. Jesus is the same yesterday, today and forever. Our loving, gracious and compassionate God is worthy of being praised!

Greg Gibson

Indeed, the Sovereign LORD never does anything until He reveals His plans to His servants the prophets.

The lion has roared—so who isn't frightened?

The Sovereign LORD has spoken—so who can refuse to proclaim His message?

Amos 3:7, 8

~ONE~

Hidden Voices

Early the next morning the army of Judah went out into the wilderness of Tekoa. On the way Jehoshaphat stopped and said, "Listen to me, all you people of Judah and Jerusalem! Believe in the LORD your God, and you will be able to stand firm. Believe in His prophets and you will succeed."

2 Chronicles 20:20

With My Father July11/2020

I asked Jesus where He wanted me to read and sensed Him directing me to John 8. I asked where He would want to meet me and felt that He was in the room with me. As I read through the chapter in John, Jesus' words from one particular verse seemed to pop off the page at me.

> Yet some of you are trying to kill Me because there is no room in your hearts for My message. I am telling you what I saw when I was with My Father. John 8:37

"Greg, sitting with Me is *the* most important thing that you can do. I spent time with My Father and you must spend time with Me. It is the only way to get a true perspective on what is taking place and where things will go. I am in control and you can trust Me to lead you in all ways. Trust Me!"

Do You Want Your Voice Released? July 18/2020

"Do you want your prophetic voice released?" Jesus asked me. This question came after sitting in the quiet and feeling like He wanted me to look over a 'word' He had given me earlier in the year about unshackling my voice.

"In many ways there is a fear in me as I think about this," I responded.

Jesus replied by saying, "Already, you are becoming aware that there must be a greater fear (reverence) of Me than a fear of what other people think of you. You must allow a reverence of Me to grow within you to such a point that you will obey My direction—and trust that they are best—over these coming days. 'For My thoughts are not your thoughts, and My ways are not your ways…' Wouldn't you agree?"

The LORD Himself watches over you!
The LORD stands beside you as your protective shade.
The sun will not harm you by day, nor the moon at night.
The LORD keeps you from all harm and watches over your life. The LORD keeps watch over you as you come and go, now and forever. Psalm 121:5-8

Position Yourself as a Speaker July 21/2020

As I was sitting with Jesus this morning, He highlighted something that a woman from our congregation spoke at the beginning of a podcast that I had recently listened to. She said that she had been learning to "position herself" as a speaker. By this she meant that it was important for her audience to know her background, training, and life story so far—the "place" from where she would be speaking.

By asking a number of questions, Jesus made it clear that it would (and will be) important to not only identify myself as a *prophetic voice* (one who hears and speaks out what he has heard from God by His Spirit) but also identify as a *watchman* (one who sees things coming before most others do) and a *gatekeeper* (tasked with not only guarding the gates of influential places and stewarding Kingdom resources, but also tasked with cleansing worship sites).

Jesus continued to speak about how positioning my voice in this way would be necessary for listeners to understand what He was saying to His Church through the voices that He was releasing, like mine. In order to connect with the audience, there must be a framing of who He has made me to be, so that a connection is made to the message that is to be spoken out.

Stay in Step August 21/2020

Reading over some of the entries in my journal, I became overwhelmed at all the LORD had spoken to me. Just as I was thinking about this, Jesus' voice broke in.

"Greg, what have I said is the most important thing to do in this season?"

"Stay in step with you," I responded.

"Then why are you anxious?" He continued. "Do you not think that you are (and have been) walking with Me over these past months? All of the time that I have given you since releasing you from your career has been in preparation for what lies ahead. You *will* be a prophetic voice. You *will* help direct My Church. You *will* be part of a great revival and harvest!

"Anxiety and fear come only when you stop focusing on Me and either fall behind or run ahead of what I have for you. Both are folly! I simply call on you to walk with Me, day by day, and marvel at how things unfold.

"Yes, writing out something like the timeline I gave you will be helpful, but only when you share and use it when and where I tell you to use it. I am giving you a new boldness to share your faith and what we have been discussing over these past weeks. I am giving you a new clarity and ability to remember and put together pieces of revelation.

"Just as you see your new church building going up, I am re-building My Church (My people) on the solid foundation of My way of doing things. There will be a closeness and dependence on Me that was never there before. *Wait, watch and wonder* is not just a motto with Me—it is a way of doing things in step with Me.

Wait – stop, call on Me, ask
Watch – listen, look for Me and where I am at work

Wonder – obediently follow Me into what I am doing in the moment. Act in the manner that I am calling you to and wonder (be amazed) at the result!"

Patience September 4/2020

I checked the spirit that I had initially been listening to in my quiet time and found it to be deceptive. As I sent it packing using the authority that I have in Christ, Jesus' voice came to me clearly.

"Greg, write this down. There is a day coming when you won't have to worry about being deceived. As My fullness settles over you, there will be no doubt as to whose presence you are in. This is not some other-worldly, heavenly thing, but a real condition on the globe.

"You wonder why I had you write about the foundation and spiritual highways of the earth; why this has not been actioned or embraced by anyone yet. You simply need to understand that you see things coming ahead of many others. What I can show you and make you understand, I cannot do to many, even though they love Me and My ways. You shouldn't get frustrated at this, for just at the right time I will release you as My voice regarding all that I have shared with you and you will not only marvel at how this all comes about, but you will be amazed at the clarity of understanding and the ability that I will give you to communicate this.

"Remember, I said to guard yourself from unbelief, as it is the enemy of hope and faith. You must be patient and endure the waiting for a time. Keep coming to Me, day and night, and you will find true rest in Me. I will provide for you in every way!"

Trust in My Words September 8/2020

"Where do you want to meet this morning?" I asked the LORD.

"Right here," He quickly responded.

"What do you want to talk about?" I asked.

"Let's talk about you. You were surprised to see in yesterday's video that key to Canada and the awakening that I am bringing forth are the passages of Psalm 24 and Malachi 4. Yet haven't I directed you to these over and over again in our times together these past years?

"Of course, others are going to hear the same plans for your nation from Me, as these haven't changed since I laid them out before the foundation of the earth. You are just beginning to deeply understand the depths of what I plan to do and yet are surprised when others point to the same markers from My Word.

"Part of walking in faith with Me is trusting in the words that I have given you. They will not give you a void return; no, they were given to increase your faith and ability/desire to follow Me *so that* you can be used for My greater glory! Trust in what we have shared together (and will share together) as none of it will be wasted. I have jealously guarded you since before you were born and I will jealously guard you moving forward!

"This is a time to get to know Me further, and with this 'knowing' will come a greater trust and a stronger faith. This will be needed in the times ahead. You feel like there is not much happening right now, but I tell you that you will look back and see all that I am doing in you (and in others) in this season, causing you all to rejoice! You can't get to where I want to take you without what I am doing in this season. Again, I say be patient. Draw close to Me and I will draw close to you. Stay steadfast! Stay alert! Continue to pray in the Spirit!

"Yes, Greg, I am coming suddenly/quickly. There will not be time to buy oil, so have your lamps full! Be dressed in your bridal clothes and continue a posture of waiting. Yes, Greg, time is short!"

God Has His Plans September 21/2020

I sat this morning, thinking about a rather disorienting conversation that I had participated in the previous day.

"Greg, you don't see what I am doing," Jesus said. "You've just spent time looking over the books you have written. Who do you think prompted you to write these? Who gave you the tenacity to stick with your writing even though you were self-publishing and things seemed to go nowhere? Would I have you do this if there was no purpose in it?

"Greg, your agitation is in seeing others shifted without realizing that I will be shifting *you*. I've clearly shown you that there is a great movement coming and that it will take many harvest workers to bring it all in. You are part of that. Just because you see no movement in your situation, no job or ministry on the horizon does not mean that it isn't just around the corner.

"Your perception of how things might unfold and how I might use you are far from what I intend for you. You are believing that you may be losing an advocate—but you can't be farther from the truth! In actuality, I am elevating those who would advocate for you and all that I have placed in you so that you will find the very niche that I have made you for.

"In fact, this is coming faster than you can imagine and you will be surprised at how it unfolds. Of course, it will be part of your story, which is such a testimony of Me! I understand the angst that you and your family are going through in this season. This is understandable and valuable. But you must not let your faith slip or your trust in all that I am doing. For just at the right time, all of this will be unveiled to you, adding to your joy!

"Greg, remember that I see the big picture!"

Ready Yourself for the Adventure September 25/2020

"Jesus, is the study the right place to meet or do you want to meet in the studio?" I inquired.

"Greg, I will meet with you wherever you are. Your voice is extremely important, both now and in the days to come. You must keep an intense focus on who I have made you to be. Every month away from your education career has served to distance the identity that you labelled yourself as, so that you could firmly and fully transition into the prophet/watchman/gatekeeper that I always intended you to be. Letting go of this former identity when you did was no accident; it has taken every day since then to transition your heart and mind to the place you find yourself in now. While there is still (and will be) some refinement to go, you are now in a place where I will be able to direct and utilize these gifts in a strong and profound way.

"You must understand and follow the timing in this if you want to enter the stream and flow of My plans for this season. Be wise and shrewd in who you share with at first. As things begin to unfold and you are sought out, you will be given leeway to say more.

"There is a pressure building as the truth of what I am doing rises under the covering of deception, chaos and unbelief. At just the right time, My plans and purposes are going to break forth, and what the enemy has sown will be lifted, as if a great fog has cleared. Like a prisoner released from solitary confinement, the great light and fresh air will be overwhelming, disorienting and shocking, as the expectation was for a longer incarceration. Many will not want to move—to embrace the 'new' reality as real. Others will refuse to see what is happening as *coming from Me* and will search for worldly explanations. Sadly, some in My Church will embrace these lies, rather than see plainly that what is happening is from Me!

"But this will not happen in your area and region if you walk obediently with Me. I will help you speak when you are called and position yourself where you are to be at the right time. This will come easier than you think! Be anxious for nothing in the days ahead, for I have positioned You exactly where I want you to be! You are a man of God, Greg, and you have proven yourself to be by your tenacity to follow Me and obey My calling for you. Get yourself ready for the adventure!"

Empathize with Leaders October 2/2020

"Jesus, what's on your heart today? What would you like to talk about?"

"Greg, you are going to have days like yesterday where you reel from the deceptive waves that crash over you unannounced. If you lose your focus on Me, what I have said is *really* happening, and the promises that I have spoken over you, you too, will be disoriented, feel hopeless and anxious about everything.

"You must come to Me daily, not necessarily for revelation (though this I will freely give you) but to stay anchored in My presence and truth. Do not blame the greater Church if they are preparing and advising others for 'a long season' of the way things are now, for their heart is to minister to others well. You would do the same thing if you didn't have the heavenly intel that I have given you for some time.

"It is good for you to know how others are tracking in this season; in order to do what I have called you to do, you must understand and empathize with the leaders you are soon going to come into contact with. As funny as it seems, your own church family will be among the hardest nuts to crack in communicating clearly this New Day and what I am doing. This is because they know you (or think they know you). They truly love you and respect you, but the message that I am delivering to them through you is hard to hear because it speaks beyond their hope and expectation right now. That is why you must wait and be in tune with expressing your message in the right moment.

"Greg, at just the right time I am going to bring you forth. You will wonder why you were anxious about this! The prophetic word you received about jumping into My river was all about this. This movement that you are a part of is way too important to Me to allow My spokespeople (like you) to flounder, and I say to you—I will make you sail! But until that day, you must cultivate your faith in such a way as to allow it to be made solid and unshakeable!

"I have chosen you to do this, Greg. I have *made you* to do this! Take comfort in the fact that I will provide everything that is needed as long as you stay focused and in step with Me. Trust what you are hearing! Be bold! Stand strong in truth! Yes, be strong and courageous!"

The Hidden Prophets October 3/2020

"Greg, let's talk about the hidden prophets. I have many (like you) hidden all across the land. I use this term so that this doesn't become about one region or nation. No, this is about My Kingdom and the glory that is about to sweep over it in great measure.

"The prayer I taught My followers was, 'Your Kingdom come *on earth* as it is in heaven' and this is exactly what I am doing in this hour. My hidden prophets are giving voice, or preparing to give voice, to this at just the right time. This does not mean that My trusted, respected prophetic voices are not speaking this—because they are. But when I release My Hidden Ones, there will be so much more impact because it will be unmistakably Me speaking through you (as well as the others)!

"I work through the humble and the least of these. My hidden voices have been faithful in spending time with Me and cultivating the kind of friendship and trust that My truth and glory can firmly rest on. Because there is no notoriety or fame in the mix, My message is spoken in a pure and innocent manner, and will be heard and understood in an unfiltered way. There will be a great impact on both believers and non-believers because of this. Remember the daisy you were shown? Purity and innocence will be a trademark of those I elevate in this season. You must seek to walk in this while you wait for Me to act.

"Yes, Greg, there is a great reward in store for those who remain steadfast, with much oil in their lamps. There is a Malachi 4 day dawning, and those who recognize this and wait and watch for it will be the first to surrender to the joy of it all. I promise, you will dance with joy!

"Be encouraged for in just a short time, all of this will break forth. My hidden prophets will be brought forward to proclaim the healing and restoration that I am surely bringing in this New Day. Do not lose heart! Be strong and courageous! Shalom!"

Jesus' Prayer October 6/2020

As I waited on the LORD, I sensed His quiet voice break into my thoughts.

"I am standing right here with you, Greg."

His right hand was on my left shoulder and He stood still, holding this position for some time in silence. My sense was that He was in a time of silent, contemplative prayer.

"Greg, I pray over you the strength and endurance to shine in this season. You are one of My forerunners, and as such you can very much direct the trajectory and influence of My Church, in a broader sense than you realize!

"I pray over you the wisdom to understand the times and the desire to follow Me into all that I am calling My Church to be. Plainly I am doing a new thing and just as the trends of the world need frontrunners to set the way for new things, so do I need those who clearly see, hear and understand what I am doing in these days to lead the way and set the new course that I am preparing for all who desire to follow Me.

"I pray for you (and the many like you) that you would have the courage to call forth this New Day for what it is—A New Day! It will only break forth as My Church proclaims and declares it as such. This is where trusting in the evidence unseen (faith!) comes in and it is the only currency that I transact in. To run on the new tracks that I have laid out for My Church, she must choose to follow Me by faith! The old tracks and the past ways will be powerless and void of life. My Bride must embrace the new wine, stored in new wineskins, in order to walk in the power and majesty of My Kingdom.

"You wanted to ask Me when healing, signs and wonders would appear to you (the Church). I tell you they are here! You simply need to believe that they are by faith. And Greg, these are not far off, but the keys to their discovery are already right here among you. You are about to open My gift to the Church—*The Book of Things to Come*—and when you do you will suddenly/quickly experience these things and more!

"Endure the season, for when you look back on this it will seem like such a short time. Those who choose to draw in to Me and seek what I am offering now will be uniquely positioned to lead the way in the days ahead. They will carry a true understanding of these times and what they mean. This is My prayer over you and My Church, and all of this will come to pass as I desire it to."

Your Assignment October 14/2020

I heard Jesus' voice say, "Just around the bend, Greg."

"LORD? What is?" came my questioning.

"Your assignment. Your engagement," His answer followed. "It's just around the corner so be patient. I am about to do a new thing and it will be hard to grasp and understand that it is happening, let alone understand that it is really Me doing this."

"How will I know what to look for?" I asked.

"When you see others coming to you for clarity and orientation, you will know it has started. And you will only be able to digest and process what you see happening in small bits. It is going to be too much for one person to understand, let alone describe and interpret for others.

"My forces have been equipped, prepared and ready for some time now. They are alertly waiting for My signal—a command to take action that all of heaven has been yearning for and to see take place. Once they begin to move there will be a quick erosion of the enemy's strongholds and fortifications. Some will come tumbling down in an instant while others will succumb to the waves of righteousness that are about to break forth!

"I tell you this so that you will continue to take seriously the preparation that is occurring in you, your family, your church and beyond. You must not relent in coming to Me—day and night—to petition Me to move in all of My fullness. This will only happen as My people, who are called by My Name, humble themselves and pray…

"You have no idea what you have been praying for in the Spirit, but that is ok. I tell you that it has been powerfully used to bring forth the movement that is set to take place. You and many, many others have been toiling to bring this forth at the right time, and that time is coming quickly! I encourage you to keep seeking Me this way.

"Greg, do not get discouraged when others do not see or hear what you are perceiving. Remember that I have you near the very front of this! It is a good thing to stay hidden in Me until the right time. Then you will be called forth to walk in the destiny and calling in which you have been made.

"Trust Me in all of this. You are hearing correctly, and so much of what I have said and promised is coming to pass shortly. Stay the course! Be encouraged! Encourage others!"

Imparting Wisdom to Others November 6/2020

As I sat thinking about the amount and strength of revelation that I received the day before, the LORD's voice broke in on me.

"You are right to think there might be a drop off in intensity and insight from yesterday if I wasn't involved… but I am!"

"Jesus, forgive me for thinking this way," I interjected.

"It's only natural when you have experienced Me in a profound way to think that it might not be the same the next time. But I tell you it all depends on your expectation and level of *believing* that you will/can meet with Me in the same way and with even more intensity! Everything depends on your attitude and faith coming into your time with Me," Jesus instructed.

"So, LORD, I sense that there is more that you want to talk about today."

"Greg, the days are getting shorter. Time is almost up."

"What do you mean by this?" I asked.

"I mean, you must get ready and follow Me in My preparation of others to support what I am doing. Don't be surprised when I have others come to you asking for wisdom. *They will come because I have sent them!* You will know beyond a shadow of a doubt because of who I send to you. They may not come to you physically, but it will be the wisdom that I have imparted to you that they will seek out, and they will simply *know* that I have given it to you.

"Do not change any details or add to what I have said; your prophetic voice must be and remain pure. This is why you must continue to go back over everything that I have told you as it all pieces together. Soon you will have the final pieces to hold on to, making the entire picture brighter and clearer. Then the encouragement that you bring to others will usher in My presence in greater measure, for others will expect Me to be present just as you have all of this time. If it wasn't for this forewarning, what you are about to experience would be too much for you!

"Stay the course! Continue to pursue Me, for in this day I can easily be found! Tell others the good news!"

Treasure in Belief November 11/2020

"LORD, I see you sitting in your chair," I said.

"Yes, Greg. Let's talk. I sent that video to you yesterday to encourage you that there are others that are tracking with Me, just as you are. In fact, there are more like you in your region than just about any other area on the planet! That should encourage you!

"I have said, 'Where your treasure is, there your heart will be also.' This is a statement of fact. If you treasure what you believe in and expect to happen ahead, your heart will be fully in it. This is why the season that you are in is so difficult for so many. Where they had their treasure is being shaken (and in some cases totally uprooted) and this is causing many, many people to lose heart. For those who know Me, some have put their faith in familiar rituals of the Church gathering and a false portrayal of who I am. This has been shaken too, and has added to the sense of disorientation.

"But you believe and know that I am coming—suddenly/quickly—in a way that will be unmistakably Me! It will take a great effort to deny not only My existence, but My sovereignty, power and omnipotence as well. Then those who have opposed Me for so long and, worse yet, have steered others away will reap an honest result. For everyone will be responsible for how they have stewarded their time and resources through this last season, especially leaders.

"Greg, trust that I have you exactly where I want you for this time. Many will be released soon to give voice, clarity and understanding to what is taking place and My intent behind it. And as the smoke clears from the battlefield, so will My prophets rise to bring guidance and direction to this New Day. Your focus must be to Me and My Word; remember all I have said to you over these past months.

"What have you just read? '…To be a friend with the world makes you an enemy of God.' (James 4:4) You cannot love the world and its ways and truly love Me. One or the other will win out. So, choose life! Choose freedom! Choose eternity!"

Power Source of the Coming Movement November 24/2020

"Good morning, LORD! Help me not to run ahead of You. My desire is to run to You and not away."

"Greg, I wish that I could show what is going on around you right now—but it is not yet time for you to see it. Be content to build your faith, your character and all that I am building into you for the days ahead.

"Yes, you have Micah and the other angels that I have sent to equip and strengthen you. When it seems in the natural that things are only moving from bad to worse, these are the times that I send My forces in to make the difference and begin the change. In reality, this change has long been started, but its manifestation in the natural will be clearly seen shortly. My known prophetic voices have been speaking to this lately, but it will be My Hidden Ones who are the power source of the coming movement. Like you, they have been communing with Me for so long, they know My heart and I know theirs! I can trust you all to complete everything I give you because you come to Me for strength rather than striking out on your own. This is why I have assigned and provisioned you with everything needed to flourish in this season, including angelic support.

"Embrace what is left in your training for soon the hiatus will be over and you will be on the move. For the Great Reversal has begun, evidenced by profound changes close to home! Yes, as this reversal comes in, you will be astounded at the complexity of it all. Yet this has been planned from the beginning!

"Trust My Spirit to lead, equip and give you wisdom while you wait for this to break forth. Our Father is faithful to give you the wisdom needed for these times and what is to come. Be encouraged! Continue to live, acting with a level mind and heart. My peace I leave with you!"

Voices in Concert December 4/2020

"LORD, why do I find it hard to come to you this morning?" I asked honestly.

"Greg, you've connected the dots between using your voice and what you know your calling is from past experiences with Me. You were suddenly reminded of how shaken you were after writing the book about Jonah and the mystery of why you were so shaken.

"But I tell you: Trust Me! If I have made you the way that I have made you and shaped you the way that I have shaped you, then don't you think that I will carry you through any task that I will call you to? I have repeatedly invited you to draw in to Me, and you have. As long as you continue to demonstrate the desire to work in concert with Me as the conductor, your efforts will bear much fruit!

"It is not just a good idea—but essential—that you go over all that I have said to you since the summer. Re-writing all of this and organizing will go a long way in helping you to remember important points and concepts in the days ahead. You must prepare for engagement with others as the opportunities that I bring forth arise. Your voice is going to work in concert with many other voices that I have placed across the country. The synergy and unison that comes from speaking boldly and prophetically will fuel the great awakening. It is the harmony in the message of many voices that bring forth the flames of faith!

"It is not a waste of time to read through what I have said; far from it! Study, study, study so that the reality of the coming movement is embedded deep in your heart. Then you will hit a second wind in your faith, endurance and understanding that no force in the heavens or earth can oppose. When I call you to the tasks that you would have shrunk back from, you will boldly step forth with confidence and trust in My call.

"Faith and obedience, equals great power!"

Organic Ministry December 9/2020

"Greg, I'm so proud of you and how you have persevered. Your steadfast devotion to keep pressing in to Me is what allows you to be used in greater and greater measure. You are about to see why this is so," Jesus said to me.

"How do you mean, LORD?" I questioned.

"Greg, the ministry that I have spoken of earlier is organic; it is birthed out of the natural shape and giftings that you were made in. Sitting with Me is like having your phone on the cordless charger; you receive more of My power, wisdom and insight each time. There will be no striving in this, no extra planning or scheming on your part. Everything you will need I will bring to you, for I am a God of provision.

"We are in partnership, you and I. And as such there will be no stopping us as long as you remain in Me and the partnership holds! Yes, as partners I hand you the keys to My Kingdom, to tear down and build up, to cultivate and to pull up. You (and the company with you) will do many works of wonder because I will it to be so! Night will soon be over and the first rays of dawn are fast approaching! Stay close to Me. Stand on the promises in My Word and those that I have made to you and that you have written down. They will have a great impact on others when I release this, and you must not be ashamed to share what we have discussed. For the day is coming when things will be flipped! It will be awkward to leave what I have done out of a conversation! Think about *that* for a minute!

"I tell you now that things are turning on a dime. The reversal is underway and at just the right time, all of this will be made apparent! I will make the wheels fall off every fake and unholy ruse to enslave My people and ultimately, their attempt to stand against Me! Those who oppose Me will be stuck—unable to move forward but way too far into all that they have done to retreat. This will become plain to the masses as more and more light breaks forth on the New Day.

"In your heart you already know this, but you must still guard what your eyes and your mind take in. Remember, precious things are occurring in the waiting, and others are following the path that you have taken. Be encouraged!"

Adding to Your Dossier December 28/2020

After two rounds of warfare prayer commanding blocking spirits that were trying to distract me from meeting with Jesus, I could finally see Him across from me as usual. He was holding the coil notepad once more. He had a pen and He seemed to be adding to the list. I just had to ask, "LORD, forgive me, but I can't recall what this list was about."

"I am adding new things to your dossier, Greg. Your spirit has been petitioning My Spirit for them in your times of prayer, and I do not withhold good gifts for My children. You are My son and I will provide you with everything needed to move forward.

Jesus continued, "You can sense that I am beginning to get you ready to move your voice forward, so that it can be prominently heard and understood. This can only come about from My doing and no amount of human wisdom or logic can make this happen. No, you are going about this the right way, even though you feel like you are blindly walking forward, not sure of what you will run into. That is ok, because it keeps you from running ahead of Me, which could be disastrous. Because I am adding to the list, you will be that much more effective when the time comes to put everything all together and voice the truth. This will be in concert with others, but I have given you a very prominent part for which I have been preparing you for all of this time.

"Yesterday was important for you and you mustn't forget that it is I who have put the righteous anger in you regarding the injustice that you see happening around you right now. I allowed you to feel some of My righteous anger so that you understand that I am not sitting idly by, allowing the enemy to run rough-shod over My people and prevent My Kingdom from coming in fullness. Wickedness will not prevail! The very fact that I am showing you that I am preparing My Hidden Ones should let you in on what I am about to do!

"Greg, stay focused on the things that My Spirit has told you to focus on. Stay the course!"

~TWO~

It's Time

For everything there is a season,
A time for every activity under heaven.
A time to be born and a time to die.
A time to plant and a time to harvest.
A time to kill and a time to heal.
A time to tear down and a time to build up.
Ecclesiastes 3:1-3

S-O-O-N October 7/2019

Jesus sat across from me, holding a box on His lap. This was a gift box and it was tied up with a ribbon that kept the lid on from all four sides. He undid the bow and opened the box, showing me what was inside. As I peered in from where I was sitting, I could see the letters S-O-O-N in solid white lettering. I knew that this meant that what was coming next was coming "soon".

I did not expect my response to this, however. There was a rise of unbelief in me and even a sarcastic flavor to it like, "Sure God, soon for you, but so much longer in the here and now." This was strong enough that I did not even write it down before leaving to take my son to choir rehearsal.

The next day I realized that I was being disobedient in not recording this and processing with Him the unbelief that surfaced with this word.

The Pocket Watch December 20/2019

After praying though a cleansing prayer, I could finally see Jesus across from me. He sat in His chair and was holding a massive pocket watch (face out) in His arms. "It's about time," I heard Him say.

As I sat there, He spoke into the delay of the permits for our church building. Unbelief wanted to pour in, so I checked the spirit speaking to me. Thankfully, Jesus doesn't mind us doing this, as He never wants us to be deceived.

It certainly was Jesus speaking, and He brought my attention back to the watch in His hands and the phrase about time. Jesus stressed that people are going to start asking me about things that He has been revealing and that my ministry would be related to this. The reason He has me write down so much of this is to keep up with what I am being taught. Jesus also cautioned me against the focusing on distraction and delay, tactics that the enemy uses to stop His messages from getting out.

Change is Imminent December 24/2019

I was praying about family matters when I suddenly noticed Jesus sitting across from me. You may wonder what this is like. The best way I can describe it is that it is like a camera coming into focus on a desired target.

As I looked at Him, I could see that Jesus was holding up a single chime. "This is to summon My angels of change," He stated. "Change is imminent."

I immediately sensed that this had much more meaning than I could grasp and that the change that was coming would be on a grand scale, as well as personal. The sudden death of our family dog days before Christmas seemed to be part of not overloading us with everything that would be shifting in the months ahead.

Chime - a bell or metal tube, typically one of a set tuned to produce a melodious ringing sound.
- to make ringing sounds, to indicate time.

Oxford Languages

Sea Change January 3/2020

On New Year's Eve, 2019, I was waiting on the LORD and saw that He was sitting across from me. He held an object in His hands that rested on His lap. As I stared at it, I could see that it was an inverted cone that appeared to be filled with water. As I asked Jesus what this was, I seemed to sense it also had something to do with time. The LORD remained silent, simply holding the cone full of liquid.

I decided to pull out my iPad and searched the two words "time-cone". Immediately I came upon a number of diagrams of what scientists call a *light cone.* With regard to defining the term, Wikipedia offered the following—"In special and general relativity, a light cone is the path that a flash of light, emanating from a single event (localized to a single point in space and a single moment of time) and travelling in all directions, would take through space."

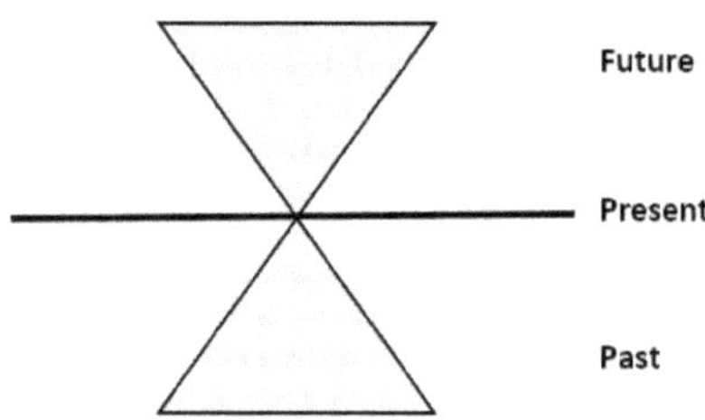

Time Cone Diagram

Three days later I was enjoying a similar time of prayer where I once again noticed Jesus in the chair across from me. He was still holding the cone filled with liquid. Once again, I thought I would ask Him what it was.

"Sea Change, Greg", came the response.

It seemed like He held the future in His hands and was about to plant it back onto the base of present/past.

I decided I had better look up the meaning of *Sea Change.* This is an idiom that means "a substantial change in perspective, especially one which affects a group or society at large, on a particular issue."

The Cambridge Dictionary defines it as "a complete change"

Merriam-Webster states that it is "a marked change or transformation."

More of Everything January 24/2020

In my morning prayer time, I knew that Jesus was present and ready, so I grabbed my journal with expectation.

"Greg, everything that has happened up to now in your life has happened to get ready for revealing the King's Highways (important spiritual corridors laid out across the earth). This is what I want them to be called and I am going to use you to introduce them to My Church.

"There is no part of anything that you have done for Me in obedience that will be wasted in this. Every part will be used for My glory. I am sending more your way, so be ready!

"Yes, Greg. More of everything! More revelation, more knowledge, more opportunities, more connections. See what only I can make happen! I am aligning your whole family in this. It is hard to see now, but soon you will see it. You (among others) will be unlocking secrets that have been hidden for ages, but are now about to be revealed. Because the time is near, these will burst forth like blossoms in the spring. Stay close to me and do not be distracted. Shalom!"

Cut to the Quick January 31/2020

I sat down to pray and looked around the room for Jesus. I asked, "Are you sitting or standing?"

"Sitting," came the response.

My eyes settled on the empty chair across from me and I could tell that Jesus was there.

"You haven't been really looking for Me lately," He commented casually, and it was true.

As I looked, I could see He was holding a dagger in His right hand. The blade was razor sharp and He held it straight up and down.

"This is to cut to the quick," Jesus stated.

I struggled to understand the idiom but could clearly sense that whatever this was referring to was time sensitive and had imminent meaning.

Cut to the Quick – to injure someone emotionally or hurt someone with words or action.

- Old English *cwic* which means alive or animated
- "Today the use of the word *quick* to mean alive is largely limited to literary author and poet. It refers to cutting through the dead parts of something until reaching the sensitive, living part of that thing."

Grammarist.com

A Gift for My Church February 10/2020

I had spent time both perusing the listening prayer practicum that I had sent a friend and pastor serving in Hobart, Australia and praying for his ministry there. At some point I looked up and noticed that Jesus was sitting across from me, waiting for me to notice Him. As I did, I saw that He was holding what looked like a large box on His knees. As I stayed with this, I noticed that it was made of cardboard, yet I sensed that there was something alive inside, though I could see no air holes. The more I looked, the more the box looked like a wrapped gift.

"This is a gift to My Church and you will soon get a chance to open it," Jesus noted.

I grabbed my journal to write this all down, after which I asked if there was anything else that He had to say.

"I am coming soon to remove the blocks to seeing Me clearly. Yes, you will all rejoice over this!"

The Gift of N-O-W April 10/2020

It was Good Friday and the day that my friend dropped off the materials for the prayer studio I plan to build in the summer. The day before I had listened to a podcast of prophets from around the world. I realized that I *needed* to look for Jesus and His comforting presence. His voice broke in but seemed diminished, so I renounced the spirit of unbelief and commanded it to leave. I looked for Jesus where He usually is, and He quickly came into focus. He had a wrapped box on His lap and immediately I saw Him pull out a word in white solid letters. It said N-O-W.

I was reminded of a previous visit when Jesus brought a similar gift with the letters S-O-O-N in it. There was a battle with unbelief at that time, too. I related S-O-O-N with what is next for me and I believe that this is true with N-O-W.

A few days later, I once again saw Jesus holding the box with N-O-W in it. I was just finishing the final proof of my latest book and the same old angst was coming over me about what to do next. He seemed to be saying that like paying for a multi-million dollar building like our church construction, starting a ministry on your own is the same. I (we) must trust that He is doing it!

I asked the LORD where I could read to confirm that I was understanding Him correctly, and felt led to read Psalm 27.

~THREE~

God's Foundation

He raises the poor from the dust and lifts the needy from the ash heap; He seats them with princes and has them inherit a throne of honor.

For the foundations of the earth are the LORD's; On them He has set the world. He will guard the feet of His faithful servants, but the wicked will be silenced in the place of darkness.

1 Samuel 2:8, 9 NIV

4:00 - "New Day Dawning" May 26/2020

After reading in Malachi, I became aware of Jesus sitting in His chair. He was holding an object which appeared to be an alarm clock. It was an old wind-up type and 4:00 was showing on the face.

I sensed the LORD prompting me to look up 4:00 in His Word. I also asked Him whether this was 4 a.m. or p.m.

"Both," came the answer.

Thinking about 4 p.m. immediately brought to my mind the parable of the man who hired workers throughout the day. Some he hired in the morning, some at noon, and others an hour before quitting time. At the end of the day, he paid them all the same wage. My sense is that we are in an hour where Jesus is preparing more workers for the coming harvest.

- 4 am = Twilight of a new day
- 4 pm = John 1:29-42 Jesus invites Andrew to spend the rest of the day with Him after asking, "What are you looking for?"
- *"New day dawning"*

4:10 - "New Day God Speaking" May 28/2020

This morning I was reviewing the May 26th vision of Jesus with an alarm clock and whether this was suitable to share during our prayer time at the River worship gathering on Sunday. Studying the John 1 passage, verse 39 jumped out at me as the two disciples responded to Jesus invitation to spend the rest of the day with Him by asking, "Rabbi, where do you live?"

The word used here means to "abide". This is the same word that is used in John 15:4 where it refers to being grafted to Jesus in a life-union.

Checking to see if this was indeed what I was to share on Sunday, I looked over to Jesus' chair and could see Him with the alarm clock, but it now read 4:10.

- 10 = made up of 4 (physical creation) and 6 (man)
  = testimony, law, responsibility and completeness of order
- John 4:10 (Jesus speaking) "If you only knew the gift God has for you and who you are speaking to, you would ask me and I would give you living water."
- *"New Day God Speaking"* Bibletools.org

5:25 - "Grace Upon Grace" June 17/2020

Sitting with my eyes closed this morning, I was suddenly aware of Jesus and the alarm clock He was holding days ago. It now read 5:25.

- The number 5 symbolizes God's grace, goodness and favor towards humans and is mentioned 318 times in Scripture. Five is the number of grace and multiplied by itself (25) is grace upon grace.
- John 1:16 "Out of his fullness we have all received *grace upon grace*." Bibletools.org

6:10 - "Manifestations of Sin Before the Law" June 23

After spending time in the Bible, I looked for Jesus. His voice broke through the silence.

"Ask me what time it is."

Before I could look, I heard 6:10. "What is significant about 6:10?" I asked.

"Many people are swinging their legs out of bed at this time. They are groggy but are taking action to start the new day. This is what is happening now.

"There must be a levelling of injustice and a building up of justice if I am to return in greater measure, not only to my Church, but other places and institutions as well. This awakening is taking place and will continue, as I 'will it' to be so," Jesus said.

- 6 = symbolizes man and human weakness, evils of Satan and the manifestation of sin
- 10 = testimony, law, responsibility and completeness of order
- *"Manifestations of sin before the Law"* Bibletools.org

3 before 7 - "Completeness Ahead of Perfection" June 25/2020

I wasn't even finished praying through my listening preparation prayer, when the LORD's voice broke in.

"Ask me what time it is now."

Instantly I knew it was 6:57 (but I thought that this couldn't be right).

"It also means that it is three minutes to seven," Jesus prompted. "There is a great awakening taking place, Greg. This is a world-wide phenomenon and not just a regional thing. It's actually 3 minutes *before* 7."

- 3 = pictures "completeness"; it is the first of 4 spiritually perfect numbers (3,7,10,12)
- "before" = in advance; ahead; in front of
- 7 = is the foundation of God's word (used 735 times) and is the number of completeness and perfection (physical/spiritual)
- *"Completeness Ahead of Perfection"*

Bibletools.org

7:24 - "Perfection of the Priesthood" June 30/2020

I prayed through the listening preparation prayer to help me to hear better. I heard a voice asking, "Quelle heure est-til? (What time is it?)"

Immediately I knew it was 7:24.

- 7 = the foundation of God's word and perfection
- 24 = is associated with the priesthood. Since it is composed of a multiple of twelve, it takes on twelve's meaning (which is God's power and authority, as well as perfect foundation) except in a higher form. 24, therefore, is also connected with the worship of God, especially at the temple.
- *"Perfection of the Priesthood"*

"Greg," He said, "worship has always been about the heart. Singing comes out of an overflow of a heart surrendered to Me. You caught yourself singing on Sunday because of this. I have not allowed singing in my temple for this season to underline this. Your heart must be surrendered to Me to fully engage in worshipping Me. Simply put: My house shall be a house of worship and prayer!"

7:55 - "God's Favor, Goodness and Grace Intensifying" July 8/2020

I spent time in repentant, cleansing prayer and then sensed that Jesus was asking me what time it was. I checked the spirit and sensed clearly that it was the LORD speaking. At first, I thought I heard 8:55 but as I stayed with this, I felt that 7:55 was correct. Jesus seemed to confirm this time.

"Greg, 7:55 is when most people are preparing to begin their work day. It is the time of day where all of their focus is on preparing for what lies ahead (immediately, for that day). Though it may not seem like it, there is a New Day fast approaching. It will be unlike anything you have ever experienced and will require all of your focus. You will be needed once this begins to steer and direct. There is an interpretation of the times that will be necessary as well. Stay close to Me and teach others to do the same."

- 7 = foundation of God's word and perfection
- 5 = symbolizes God's grace, goodness and favor towards humanity
- 55 = is a connotation of the double influence of the number 5 and therefore symbolizes the intensity of the grace that God has for all of His creation.
- *"God's Favor, Goodness and Grace Intensifying"*

Bibletools.org

12 after 8 - "God's Power and Authority Following a New Beginning" July 14/2020

I read through Matthew 13-15 as I felt that was where Jesus was leading me to study. When I looked at the chair where He usually sits to meet with me, I sensed He was there with the alarm clock once more. As I looked at the face of the large clock, I read and heard at the same time, "12 after 8".

- 12 = a perfect number
  = symbolizes God's power and authority, as well as a perfect governmental foundation; completeness
- After = in the time following; behind; succeeding

- 8 = new beginning, a new order or creation; man's true 'born again' event
  = symbolizes circumcision of the heart
- *"God's Power and Authority Following a New Beginning"* Bibletools.org

8:12 - "Creation of God's Perfect Government Foundation Completed" July 20/2020

I spent some time reading and praying through the listening prep prayer. I asked where I should read in His word and got nowhere, so I looked for Jesus in the room. I immediately sensed Him in the chair across from me.

"Ask Me what time it is," I hear Him query.

As I looked and listened, I sensed 8:12. I thought, "This can't be right. This is the same time that it was when I looked before." So, I sat with this, soon realizing two things: 1. God operates outside of time, 2. Jesus was telling me that it was 8:12, a different take on the "12 after 8" that He had shown me on July 14th.

- 8 = New beginning; a new order or creation
- 12 = God's power and authority; perfect governmental foundation; completeness
- *"Creation of God's Perfect Government Foundation Completed"* Bibletools.org

It's Time July 31/2020

I sat in the study asking Jesus where He wanted to meet. Immediately I sensed Him in His chair holding the alarm clock.

"It's time," I heard Him say.

I could no longer see the hands on the clock—it was like they were no longer there. Jesus arms and hands rested on the outer casing of the clock, His hands near His chin.

"Greg, from this point on things are going to change rapidly. Your assignment and what I have in store for My Church are one in the same. All of the things that you have heard from Me and through the voice of the prophets are coming to pass: Fear of the LORD, proclaiming the Kingdom, boldness to stand for Me, freedom from addictions, signs and wonders. All of this is not only starting but is about to gain great momentum.

"You are alarmed at this, thinking that you don't have a suitable building (at St. Albert) at present to house this. But I tell you that this will spill out *from within you* as you go and be the Church…

"It's called an alarm clock because it is meant to awaken you from your slumber—an abrupt call to move from inactivity to a New Day and all that comes with this fresh beginning. *This is a New Day*, and you will not want to go back to the way things were… Trust Me!"

Reasons for the Timeline August 31/2020

"Why did I give you that timeline, Greg?" Jesus asked.

"So that we would know that a New Day has indeed started. Yet if I go anywhere near what the media is saying or out to buy something, there is another narrative being played out," I responded.

"So, I ask you again, why is the timeline important?"

"Jesus, I believe it is a declaration of your sovereign favor and grace over your people. This New Day has already started, but to see it we must look through the eyes of faith. The enemy is doing his best to cover Your glory from being seen—but this is an impossible feat and he knows it!" I answered.

"Yes, if you look strictly through human eyes you would absolutely miss what is really transpiring in the Spirit," Jesus added. "My Church must be a Spirit-led

Church, and you must allow Me to show you what is really transpiring in the unseen realm. Satan is deceptively and desperately trying to hold this false covering in place, but the Winds of Change are too strong for this to last for long. But be aware that after the corners are lifted and light has poured in, fear will still have a stronghold for a time. This thought settling (fear of unseen danger) over the people has been reinforced via mask wearing and will take some time to recover from. Remember, "Perfect love casts out all fear" and it is My perfect love that comes with My glory. All of this is available *now* to My Church."

"Jesus, how do we access this?" I asked.

"The more time you spend with Me, the more you will see things as they really are. Many of you saw Me coming to My Church as King a while back and this is certainly happening now!

"My glory rests on a few who are currently looking for Me. There are many more who are awakening to My presence because of the interruption to 'normalcy' the pandemic has brought. Think about crowd surfing. If only a few have their hands up, the person over the crowd will be dropped. I tell you, My presence is much heavier than this! Therefore, I am looking for My Bride to not only look for Me, but posture themselves in such a way that they may carry My glory to a world that desperately needs hope! This is what is happening in this hour!"

Building a True Foundation September 5/2020

I drove to St. Albert and to our church site that was under construction to pray.

"Well Jesus, you came along with me today. What is on your heart?" I asked.

"Greg, do you see how everything is taking shape? The form of the building can now be seen and this is a picture of what I am doing in My people (the Church) during this season. You thought you had a solid foundation to build from, but just look at how much ground work has to be done in order to have a parking lot that is solid and can withstand the weight of everything that will roll on to it.

"Well, I'm coming in more fullness and a weightier presence than you have ever experienced before! Without a significant personal foundational upgrade, My Bride would not be able to hold My presence and all that I plan to do in and around your church, and beyond. The former will be much less than the latter and this will be something to celebrate! Continue to encourage and pray for others until they begin to see this too!"

~FOUR~

Wheat, Weeds and the Harvest

The kingdom of heaven is like a farmer who planted good seed in his field. But that night as workers slept, his enemy came and planted weeds among the wheat, then slipped away.

The farmer's workers went to Him and said, "Sir, the field where you planted the good seed if full of weeds! Where did they come from?"

"An enemy has done this!" the farmer exclaimed.

"Should we pull out the weeds?" they asked.

"No," he replied, "you'll uproot the wheat if you do. Let both grow together until the harvest. Then I will tell the harvesters to sort out the weeds, tie them into bundles, and burn them, and put the wheat in the barn."

Matthew 13:24-26

The Winnowing Fork August 21/2019

Today I was asking Jesus about whether I should apply for a part-time teaching position. As I looked to Him, Jesus was sitting in His chair, with something about a foot and a half long that He held vertically, like a baton. As I gazed at this, the term "winnowing" came to my mind and I knew that this was a tool for harvest, a winnowing fork. I was reminded of John the Baptist's words:

> "I baptize with water those who repent of their sins and turn to God. But someone is coming soon who is greater than I—so much greater that I am not worthy even to be His slave and carry His sandals. He will baptize you with the Holy Spirit and with (in) fire. *He is ready to separate the chaff from the wheat, with His winnowing fork*. Then He will clean up the threshing area, gathering wheat into His barn but burning the chaff with never-ending fire." Matthew 13:11, 12 (emphasis mine)

Impartation and Amplification September 11/2019

We were praying at the church building as a prayer team. I sensed the LORD sitting with us, His hands and arms were out, fingers up and palms out. I heard Him speak to me, "Impartation, Greg."

"On us?" I queried, thinking of the four people in the room.

"On you and many others. This will happen quickly and soon. You will see it in your day-to-day, prayer and love for others." There was a pause, I then heard Him say, "Amplification. I am turning things up and you will have and receive even more of Me. Greg, it is time for My Bride to take Me seriously! There is a time coming suddenly/quickly when it will be too late for some. As I reveal more and more of myself, there are those who choose to step away from Me. I wish this was not so, but you can pray that this would be lessened."

Winnowing Shovel October 13/2019

After asking Jesus where He would want to meet, I noticed Him leaning against the cat perch across from me. As I looked at Him, I saw a longer, flat object that He held in His right hand that half-rested against His thigh. Quickly I observed that it wasn't a sword, but something made primarily of wood. Once again, the term "winnowing" came to my mind, though this object seemed to be more like a shovel than it did a fork.

> "Likewise, the oxen and donkeys which work the ground will eat seasoned fodder, which has been winnowed with shovel and fork." Isaiah 30:24 NKJV

Discussing Unbelief May 11/2020

Yesterday as I sat with Jesus, I could see Him sitting across from me in priestly garments. He began to speak to me, telling me that I would be in a much different role a year from now. For a number of reasons, I let that just dissolve, and I moved on to other things.

Today I was with Jesus again, asking what the main thing was that most affected my connecting with Him.

"Unbelief" came the answer. "Greg, do I ever not speak the truth to you?"

"Of course not," I replied. "What you tell me is always true."

"Yet there are times that what I have spoken or said to you is received with unbelief in your heart. Further, you are still afraid that I will ask you to do something you won't want to do."

"Yes, this is true, even though I know that if you do this, you always have something better ahead," I admitted.

Jesus remained silent as I thought about a job change that He had asked me to willingly take on. "LORD, you knew things about that situation that I did not know. And you fast-tracked my retirement so that I could enjoy three more months of "normalcy" as well as have extra time to sit with you and write."

Jesus sat across from me, smiling. "The more that you are in My Word and know My character—who I really am—the less unbelief you will struggle with."

Wheat and Tares June 11/2020

I asked Jesus if He was sitting or standing, and couldn't discern either. Finally, I had a sense that He didn't want to meet with me where He usually sits in the room, but elsewhere. An image of Jesus came to me, and He was standing on the unfinished platform of the studio my son and I were building that overlooks the valley at our acreage. Jesus was facing west across the basin with His hands up. This reminded me of Moses standing to part the Red Sea.

"I am dividing the wheat from the tares, Greg. This will cause great division but it is necessary for these times."

Understanding the Times August 8/2020

After checking the spirit(s) that I had been listening to, the voice of the LORD came to me.

"I'm sitting so I want to teach you," He said. "Why do you think that I have been coming to you and showing you different themes?"

"I believe that you are trying to communicate what you are doing and what you have in store ahead for your Church."

"And why would it matter that My people understand what is happening in these times?" He went on asking.

"I think it is so that we respond and partner with the angels You are sending to bring renewal. If we don't understand what you are doing and how to respond the way that you want us to, then this 'move' will be much less effective than you intend. Your pre-creation design for this has not changed and we must fit into these plans in order for it to be all that you intend it to be."

"So, what does this involve," He asked again.

"First, we have to have the *faith* to see, hear and believe in this plan from the beginning. Then, as more of us see it *and believe it*, we must follow you obediently, step by step into it. We must see past the 'current events' and situation that is clouding our hearts and minds with unbelief, and look with spiritual eyes at what You are doing."

"Greg, because you are a watchman, you are one of the first to see this coming. But you are not alone and very soon others will be joining with you to usher in an understanding of what is transpiring, as My glory moves into homes, communities and regions to a greater degree. You are learning to 'press in' to Me in order to understand what is on My heart and what I am doing in this hour. This is a very good thing! Rejoice, and again I say, rejoice! For healing is coming to your house!"

The Era of the Harvest August 17/2020

I wondered if the LORD was in His chair as I settled down in the silence of the morning.

"Greg, I will meet you every day here if you are willing to meet."

I responded with, "LORD, you have been so gracious to me! You have been sharing some very deep and intricate plans for the days ahead."

"That is because the world has never seen what I am bringing forth. You know that there is a great harvest of souls coming, where many will dedicate their lives fully to Me. This can only take place if My Kingdom and glory draw closer. To do this, there must be those whose lives will host the very essence of My being—true followers!

"You were right that before I started My ministry on earth, John the Baptist was paving the way, leading those who would bow in repentance. Any true harvest of souls must first be preceded by a wave of repentance. For there must be a turning away from the things that ensnare us and keep us from true worship and adoration, in order to authentically turn to Me and see Me."

"How does your Church navigate the difference in the current physical reality and what is taking place in the Spirit?" I asked.

Jesus sat smiling at me with His hands out and palms up. "I sent 'the seventy' out to proclaim the Kingdom had arrived with their hands empty. Nothing has changed. You (My Church) are to do the same. If you have the faith to declare this New Day and that My Kingdom is advancing, you will see the signs, miracles and healings that you have read and dreamed about. You will read and hear about other places where this is breaking out. It will only happen where people truly believe that I have poured out a new wine in a new wineskin and that My heavenly armies have moved in. In every instance, it will be because My Kingdom has been authentically and whole-heartedly proclaimed *and that this is the era of the harvest*—if you seek Me, you will find Me!"

"But how does this happen if we are not gathering together in-person?" I queried.

"I will tell you again that My glory rests on anyone who truly believes that I come to them in spirit and in power, and who believes by faith that I am coming in My sovereignty to advance My Kingdom over all of the earth. As long as there is a faithful remnant who posture like this in a community, My presence can and will rest there.

"Now you can see that the real reason for angling your local church building wasn't so much that the building could be used during construction as much as it represents the new alignment to Me and My ways. Each of My followers who have been spending Spirit-led time with Me will be like diesel-soaked logs to a fire when you return to meeting together. They will set anyone near them ablaze in the Spirit by what they carry from spending time with Me. In the meantime, this will also happen as My worshippers interact by the current means available. Do not give up praying together, as this is where much of this faith transference is taking place!"

The Latter Rain August 22/2020

I sat with Jesus in the study and we watched the rain fall outside the window together. Everything looked so green and lush, and the Mountain Ash tree near the house was loaded with clumps of bright orange berries.

"Why does the rain fall on some places and not on others?" He asked me. "My latter rain is going to fall in places where you would not expect, and other spots (that would seem like profitable places for renewal) will not. There are reasons for this and are part of My mysterious plan laid out before time.

"Greg, there is no other time of the year when your yard is so full of life. Every leaf has reached its potential;

new limbs have stretched out. The birds and animals and insects all thrive. All because of the time of year—the season that is here.

"It is like that now in the spiritual reality. All of the conditions are favorable for growth, vitality and maturity. Everything points toward the coming harvest. I bring rain to appointed places at appointed times. Everything in nature obeys My will and My commands. As My people learn to follow and obey Me like this, so too, will the latter rain fall to bring about all that I want to accomplish in the time ahead. Do not lose heart, as this has already begun!" (See Joel 2:23-29)

Separating the Wheat from the Tares November 8/2020

"Do you think that the faith of My people is being strengthened right now?" asked Jesus. "You have just read through My list of faith champions and what did you see? You saw examples of people standing on the reality of what they *knew* I had told them!

"This is a time when you will see the wheat and the tares separate. Those who have been truthfully drawing in to Me will continue on. They will gain strength in standing on the foundation of what I have spoken and highlighted from My Word. Others will choose to listen to what is being sent their way as 'truth'.

"Greg, you cannot have it both ways. Either what the world tells you is truth or what I say is the truth—the two are in opposition to one another. Therefore, pray for My Church to rise up and truly hear and understand what I am doing in this hour, for the sad fact is that there will be those who decide to leave Me, despite My impending approach and how near it is.

"But you have been steadfast; you have obeyed My call and instructions, and have embraced what I have been doing to distance you from the storm so that you could see and hear clearly. Pray for others, that they would not be blown away by the Winds of Change. Pray for those who are disoriented and having trouble finding traction with the truth and what I am doing. Pray for your church leaders, that they would look for the guidance of My Spirit like never before, for this is the only way to navigate through the storm of deception.

"Greg, wear your prophetic hat. Be who I've called you to be! Speak out what I have clearly said to you as the Church is going to need many beacons of light to keep from crashing on the rocks of despair. Don't give up on the New Day, for it is approaching suddenly/quickly! Continue to guard your faith, for I tell you that it is powering a great movement!"

Dismantling False Movements December 3/2020

Jesus' voice broke in and He began to again speak about a coming separation of people groups.

"Greg, the powers and principalities of the earth are about to lose much of their strength. I have been dismantling and tearing down the support of their human networks and this soon will become very evident.

"This will transpire in unison with My glory moving forward into all facets of culture and the organizations of the earth. That is why there is a great time of revelation and exposure taking place on the earth right now. Those who have willingly aligned themselves with the agenda of the demonic powers will be forced to stand up and be counted—one way or the other. This is the true division taking place right now—not the false movements of political or racial division. Both of these movements have at their core very real issues that need to be dealt with in a righteous way, just not as a front for covert ends to an evil agenda.

"The retreat of Satan's forces along with the advance of My armies will make room for a multitude of miraculous occurrences and seemingly impossible turn-arounds. The New Day is bringing with it everything that is not currently evident in this season: hope, expectation, joy and faith! These things will not only hold up and support My Kingdom, but they will cause all things to thrive as well."

The False Narrative vs. A Holy Awe December 23/2020

After reading Joshua 1-3, Exodus 15 and Job 1 and 2, I looked for Jesus. I could see Him comfortably resting across from me holding a modern pen and coil note pad.

"Why are you showing me the note pad, LORD?" I just had to ask.

"Greg, I'm here to encourage you. It is not easy to stay in step with Me and who I am in the midst of the Great Storm. I am listing all the ways you have stuck with it—remained in a strong state of relationship with Me so that I can prepare you for what is ahead. I know the unique gifting and shape that you have—I put it there—but I also know how difficult it is to share some of the burdens that come with this.

"Soon however, your task *will be* to share with others, and you will need all of the boldness, courage and faith that I have been building in you since before you finished your teaching career. But as the waters begin to recede and you feel the momentum shifting, I will infuse into My followers a supernatural strength as your faith builds. Many of My believers are beginning to understand that the only way out from under such great oppression is a mighty miracle from Me. Giants own the land right now, empowered by supernatural forces. But even these were all made by Me *and must submit to My sovereignty when I act—*

and act I shall! There is a full-on rebellion taking place and the Lord of Hosts is being mocked!

"I have made lists of many things, as nothing gets by Me; nothing can remain in the shadows without Me noticing it. Just like the Christmas lists so many people have made, I have made My lists and they are thorough and comprehensive. When I act it will be a Red Sea moment! All of the nations of the world will know that there is only one God and there will not be one person who does not see My power for what it is! Who else can strangle the strongholds that have moved against My people with such force? Only the sovereign God of the universe! Only I have the power to make Red Sea and Jordan River moments!

> He (God) did this so all of the nations of the earth might know that the LORD's hand is powerful, and so you might fear the LORD your God forever. Joshua 4:24

"This reversal from the fear of the virus and the narrative being told, to transitioning to the holy awe of the LORD, will be greatly disorienting. Many will want to believe in the false narrative that they have been told over these past months, but I will be calling forward those who can bear My presence to stand in the Jordan and allow Me to create a way forward for My people. I want to bring them clarity and vision in this day; to shake off the fog that the manipulation, intimidation and control that has come over them from such overt amounts of witchcraft. You aren't necessarily one of these, but you are to encourage other leaders to stand and uphold My presence so that the ugly waters of the storm can be parted. My people *will be* allowed to cross into the New Day! When My people crossed the Jordan, it was the season of harvest, just as it is now. In the natural, it seemed impossible to cross given the river was in flood, just as it seemed impossible to escape Pharaoh and his mighty army. But I tell you I have a way forward from this, and what seems like an impossibility is, in fact, about to happen!

"Greg, I see all that you have done to draw into Me. It is impossible for Me not to notice! Walk out these remaining days of waiting like you have victory because you do! Hold on to the promises I have given to you, for they will not be taken away from you. Encourage others, remain steadfast and in My Word. For you all are about to rejoice like you never have before!

"Wait, watch and wonder!"

Look to the Son December 24/2020

Last night when I was up meeting with Him, the LORD mentioned three things that I became aware of while I was praying in the Spirit.

- Look to the Son.
- Prepare the ground.
- Deliver us from the evil one.

I looked for Jesus and saw that He was holding a bowl that was more cone-shaped than it was round. I knew that it held the prayers of the saints.

"I have heard the prayers of My people, Greg. They have been crying out to Me—day and night—from all parts of the world. They have tipped the scales and everything that takes place in the coming days will be like the Exodus. I am removing the influence of Egypt and freeing My people to truly worship Me. And unlike the small remnant of non-Israelites that left Egypt as well, there will be a great multitude from all nations that come into My Kingdom in the days and months ahead.

"Yes, Pharaoh is being stripped of everything he thought he controlled and owned—nothing will be left to him. Even the dates he thought he was setting will be Mine to set, says the LORD! All the wealth that he and his cohorts stockpiled and counted on will be given over to My people and for righteous purposes. None of that will be left to them. Great fortunes will be gone in a single day. As these false empires and kingdoms fall, there will be great rejoicing throughout the earth. Then My Church will arise in such a way that has never been seen before and never will again on this present earth. It will be a time of great harvest, and the bulk of My workers will be those who have recently been rescued from disaster! They will serve Me with vigor and zeal, and the difference in My people will be tangible because of this!

"Continue to look to the Son! He will lead in this day and will be victorious! Guard your eyes and do not stray from what I have promised you. Stay in step and encourage everyone that you come in contact with."

~*FIVE*~

Harps and Angel Armies

Praise the LORD, you angels,
you mighty ones who carry out His plans,
listening for each of His commands.
Yes, praise the LORD,
you armies of angels who serve him
and do his will!
Praise the LORD,
everything He has created,
everything in all His kingdom.
Psalm 103:20-22

Jesus and His Harp April 1/2019

We were praying together at the church. As I waited on Jesus, I began to see Him sitting on the stool in front of me (in the middle of our circle of chairs). Jesus was resting with His feet out and at an angle (feet together) yet His posture was casual. I began to see that He was holding a harp. Thinking that this was somewhat weird, I checked the Spirit speaking to me and it certainly was Him. Jesus brought my attention back to the harp.

"It has been a while since I talked to you about angels. This is what I use to summon them. With every note struck come My angels specific to the assignment that I am calling them to. Why do you think that I am showing you this?" He asked.

"It is because you are summoning angels here and it seems like there are many called," came my response.

"And why do you think that this is so?"

"I believe that you are saying there will soon be a need for more personal and corporate angels."

"And yes," Jesus responded, "there will be many encampments; more than you can imagine!"

Summoning Angels August 29/2019

As I sat with the LORD, I could see Him sitting in the chair across from me, holding His harp. He asked me, "What would happen if I summoned my angels?"

I had trouble discerning what He was getting at, so I checked the spirit speaking to me. It was the LORD. So, I asked to be able to linger with this question and for Him to help me to understand this. "Is it better to travel during a time of peace or a time of war?" He inquired.

I began to think of the Allied armies pushing the Nazi forces back to Germany during World War II. They had greater numbers and strength, but the Nazi's fought them at each town and major roadway intersection. It was evident who was going to win, but the enemy stubbornly held on to ground until forced off, defiling it and destroying important structures in its wake.

A few days later, Jesus' voice broke in again on the subject of His harp. "I use the harp for reconciliation of sound defilement. My angels respond immediately to its notes bringing full restoration at My command. This has been happening during this season and that is why you are seeing the water table restored in your area. Nothing supersedes the notes I have struck and they cannot be reversed. My dominion will be experienced throughout the whole earth!"

The Wind of Angels March 7/2020

Just before the Covid-19 crisis set in, we held a three-day spiritual freedom conference at the church I attend. As part of the pray support team, I was standing at the back of the sanctuary as the worship set neared its completion on the opening day. In an instant I began to see many spiritual beings flying around the room, like swallows. I could tell that their movement was doing something to the spiritual atmosphere around us.

I was reminded of Psalm 104:4 that states: "He sends His angels like the winds, His servants like flames of fire."

Angelic Foundation May 30/2020

I spent some time writing out and sending what I felt God had been saying to me over the forty days of Pentecost. When I finished, I looked up and sensed Jesus sitting across from me and holding His harp.

"Ask Me to send more angels to your church site and the men that you sent the journal entry to," came His request.

I prayed that very thing and quickly broke into praying in the Spirit. As I prayed, I could see Him slowly strum the strings of the instrument on His lap. I found myself praying, "More, more, more…" repeatedly. I could see the frame of the new building going up in my mind and called to the LORD to send more angels to fill the space.

Jesus broke in saying, "I have already laid the foundation."

Angel Legions June 12/2020

I began my time asking Jesus where He wanted to meet.

"Right here," came the answer.

"What's on your heart?" I asked Him.

"What's on your harp?" Jesus quipped. Once again, He was directing me to notice His harp. "Greg, I have many legions of angels ready for deployment in your area. Many have been hand-picked "special-ops" forces. The awakening that is coming will begin with only a handful of people, but this will be more than enough. Continue to encourage others to fully commit to Me.

"There will be a falling away of many who once said that they stood for me. Do not despair, this happened to My early group of disciples as well. Some will return to Me. This is what I was talking about when I spoke of the Winds of Change and the Wheat and the Tares. My holy presence is coming to My Church in a much stronger way when we return and not all will be able to stand in it. There is much refining that must take place before this happens."

"But LORD," I interjected, "what are the angel legions for?"

"They will be released when you learn to stand in My presence and depend fully on My Spirit. Then the signs and wonders some of you have asked for will be common-place, as the Church learns to truly partner with Me. Trust that I am doing a new thing, Greg, and I will not reverse this. There is no going back! The tunnel is short and there is a great light waiting ahead. Remember the prophecy given to you about the River of Joy that you swam in? Well, it leads to My throne! Know this: time is short."

An Angelic Garrison August 1/2020

I felt Jesus leading me to meet Him at our studio that overlooks the valley and the rest of our property. I asked Jesus why He wanted to meet with me there.

"Greg, look with your eyes *open*," He said.

I could see that there were all kinds of activities happening throughout the area—many, many beings lifting off and landing. It reminded me of a Vietnam War base with helicopters coming and going, but was much more. In addition, there was much angelic activity on the ground.

Jesus' voice broke in saying, "They are getting ready for deployment up and down My highways. In many ways this is a military move. With My presence comes My glory and the two are inseparable. If My Church is to have more of Me, then there must be suitable preparations made or you would not be able to be near My presence. These special forces have been released to make way for more of Me. I'm allowing you to see this so that you can explain to others what transpired *before* My presence became so real to them!"

"Is that my future assignment? I asked.

"That is part of it."

More on the Garrison August 2/2020

I decided to meet with Jesus on our back deck that overlooks the valley. "What's on your heart today?" I questioned the LORD.

"Let's just talk, Greg."

"What do you want to talk about?"

"Why do you think that I have been showing you the Garrison again?" He inquired.

"It is important for the days ahead," I guessed.

"Exactly. Your experience seeing this years ago with others and the validation of these visions at the prophetic school you attended were meant to help you *believe* all that I have been showing you as of late. This not only ties into your destiny but the destiny of the local Church.

"There is a disorientation in My people that I am about to take away, bringing both clarity and vision. You would think that this would be a good thing. Yet with this comes a temptation to act out of alignment with Me and before it is time. There must be an obedience to wait on Me for directives and timing! Running ahead can be disastrous and My Church must learn to stay in step with Me. This must be the message that stays in the forefront in the weeks and months ahead!"

A Great Offensive is Coming August 20/2020

"I'm sorry, LORD, but I don't have a chair for you," I said. I was sitting in the lone chair in my partially finished prayer studio that we were building.

"You will soon. What do you see?" He asked me, gazing through the glass patio doors we had recently installed.

"I see the Garrison and much activity. It's like your army is getting ready (or is already engaged) in a major campaign."

Jesus now stood right at the glass doors and continued with His thoughts.

"My army is caught in the 'now, but not yet' stage of the movement. My angels have been in position for a long time, but it is My people who I am waiting for. My angelic army always partners with My people in faith. Without faith, you can do nothing!

"There is a great movement coming and it is this movement that has all of heaven on its feet. A great offensive is coming—is here—that will take down enemy strongholds and build fortresses of righteousness. You and those that you meet with will be a great part of this.

"The action you see taking place in the spirit is but only the start of all that I have planned for this season. This (angel) activity will only increase as My followers awaken to the power that dwells within them by My Holy Spirit."

> I called on the Lord, who is worthy of praise, and He saved me from my enemies. Psalm 18:3

Angelic Generals September 3/2020

"Let's meet in the studio today, Greg."

Even though I was in the room that we call the study in our house, I felt like I could meet with Jesus "in the Spirit" staying right where I was.

"Look and see," I heard Him say.

I could tell that Jesus was sitting in the studio where I usually sit, with three others in the chairs around Him. There was a fourth being there, standing by the door and who seemed to be scribing what was taking place.

"These are the generals for this region," Jesus noted. "They are receiving final instructions from Me before I release them. They come from other garrisons in the area, but yours is rather strategic. Some of this has to do with the amount of cooperation and partnership we have with you. To do what they are called to do, they need high levels of prayer and endorsement. Your obedience in not only building the studio, but using it for My glory lends naturally to a faith that can be used to advance My presence. Others are acting and obeying like this as well, throughout this country and the rest of the world.

"You, however, are a frontrunner and a pioneer; this is a place that we can use to launch the righteous offensive that so many have been waiting for. This is why all of heaven has been leaning forward, to watch and encourage as this movement takes hold."

I paused to look at the studio and what Jesus was doing. I could see that He was now standing and as I watched, He was giving each general a brand-new, gleaming two-edged sword. This was done ceremonially and with real intent. I could tell that these swords were made specifically for the strengths of each one of them and for such a time as this. I could not tell whether these were angelic beings or humans brought here in the Spirit.

"Each of My generals has a specific part to play in the coming movement. They each will be integral pieces in what is about to unfold. I want you to pray (along with others) for them, that their missions would be completely fulfilled. This is an important part of your assignment in these next few weeks. Be faithful! Be steadfast! Run the race as it is meant to be run!

Kneeling Angelic Warriors September 14/2020

This morning (in the studio) I looked at Jesus sitting across from me. He was dressed very regally and had His scepter. As I glanced out the glass doors, it seemed like there were hundreds (if not thousands) of angelic warriors, all down on one knee, facing where I was sitting.

I asked Him, "LORD, why are you showing me this?"

"Greg, I want you to grasp how ready I am to move with My army at this hour. All the preparations are over; My forces await their orders to move out and they are anxious to begin!

"What you see here (the whole field as far as I could see populated with a kneeling, totally submissive army) is but a small representation of My forces. This garrison has much strength because of generations of prayer for what is coming. You have been called as a part of this, but the petitions of many, many others set all of this in motion. This has been part of My plan from the beginning.

"Would you be sitting out here this morning without Me? Would you be observing this now without the obedience of your friend in bringing you the material? And what about your will to build and finish the studio on time? Who placed that within you? I tell you that you will see much more of this kind of thing in the days ahead!

"You have been given only a glimpse of the infrastructure known as the King's Highways. But in the days ahead, I will reveal more of this to My Church so that those that you see kneeling before Me will have all of the support they need to be successful in all that I call them to as My glory spreads throughout the earth.

"Greg, don't get tired of waiting. For in the waiting, you are finding great treasure and it will not be taken from you. And don't get weary of telling others that there is blue sky coming, because it is!"

The Great Reversal November 9/2020

After praying for some time in the Spirit, I suddenly noticed Jesus sitting in His chair. Once more He had His harp in His lap.

"LORD, I know that you use your harp to summon your angels for your purposes. Is there a significance to you showing me this today?"

"Greg, the strings are silent now because My notes of command have already been sent out to My angelic legions. The angels that were ready for My signal have now been dispersed and their mission will not be reversed or repelled. This is a landmark day, for I have heard the pleas of My saints and I will not turn away from them!

"Soon you will begin to see with your own eyes the Great Reversal; the first shall be last and the last, first. I am upsetting the order of many things, so much so that you may wonder if the end is near. But take heart, it is not!

"I told you that the storm needed to occur to shake all things loose that could be shaken. It is in its final stages now and there is much pollution, anxiety and tension everywhere because the forces of good and evil are both equally allowed to move freely during this time. But understand that with the release of My legions the tide is swiftly turning! Where there was chaos and open insurrection, I am bringing clarity, order and truth. The reversal of *what was* is beginning as we speak.

"What have I told you? There is a New Day dawning that is escorting My glory into all of the earth! Could this happen if the forces of darkness were allowed to rule the day with deception and lies? Of course not! I have spoken to you much about your faith because you must stand on what I have told you, regardless of what you see in the natural. The reasons we are having these visitations and recording what I have said is not only to build your faith now, but for the weeks and months ahead. This is where the real growth will take place! Many, many others will benefit from this as well.

"Greg, look to Me for the truth and then walk in it!"

Clearing the Way December 6/2020

We spent time, Jesus and I, discussing thoughts I had been getting regarding the virus, the pandemic and all of the trouble it had caused and who, if any, could be held responsible for it. Jesus simply tracked along with My thoughts as I went from one thing to another, stopping to pray, then moving on to the different questions that I had. Somehow, I knew it wasn't the time or the place to record these thoughts.

Suddenly, I realized that Jesus was holding His harp and was rhythmically strumming the strings across its full breadth. He began to speak as he did this.

"My entire angelic army has been released unto the ends of the earth. They are overwhelming strongholds that once empowered the enemy's agenda, but are now falling to forces of righteousness, justice and holiness. This is a world-wide phenomenon and there is no place that these effects will not be felt.

"Greg, like the tide receding they are causing the Great Reversal. Things are returning to the way that I created them to be—at least for a while. This long wait in exile these past months has ripened the harvest fields. These angels are preparing the way for this great time of reaping! This is why you and others too, have been perceiving just how busy My Church will be in welcoming, teaching, discipling and sending out the mass of true followers that I am sending to her. This almost seems inconceivable to you now, but shortly it will be the reality! Look again at today's verse:

> Our great desire is that you keep on loving others as long as life lasts, in order to make certain that what you hope for will come true. Hebrews 6:11

"As I have spoken of before, the Great Storm was intended to suffocate out the hope and expectation in My people that leads to faith. But like all that he does, the enemy has overplayed his hand, and it has been that very thing that is now giving birth to a *movement* of faith and expectation!

"So, I assure you, My armies are at work and fueled by the power of the prayer of the saints, clearing the way for the presence of the LORD! My glory is breaking forth and is even now spreading across the earth. Yes, just like in an actual new day, this movement is rising in the east and making its way across the globe. Be patient! Dawn is breaking shortly over you! Trust in everything that I have said and have yet to tell you. Love those around you and encourage them!"

Angelic Forces Overwhelming Strongholds Dec. 16/2020

"Deployed, Greg. My forces are deployed."

This came after reading Psalm 64 and thinking about how I used to pray in the studio when the weather was warmer. I sensed the angelic garrison on our property that was full to overflowing this fall and emptied to maintenance levels. I heard Jesus begin to speak again.

"Greg, all of My forces have been sent to key positions around the country. These are surprise raids on strongholds that the enemy felt that they had uncontested control over. But I tell you overnight their grounds were revoked so that My forces could move in righteousness and light. Every evil and cunning scheme is coming to light, so much so that those who have felt secure in their secretive network are stunned to the point that they can hardly think, let alone act. Fear has reversed itself onto those who were only a short time ago, promoting fear over the masses.

"My angelic forces are overwhelming so many important strongholds so quickly and efficiently, there has been no time to cover evidence or tracks. Everything is being laid bare for what it was. All of this will testify against the absolute evil that was being prepared for the days ahead."

"What about those law enforcement officials who are faithful to the law and upholding justice?" I interjected.

"I have always had the right people in the right places, but now is the time to act. Those that I have raised up to stand strong and not shrink back are doing so now! I predestined them to be exactly where they are now so that My will would be swiftly and efficiently carried out."

Jesus continued, "As this evil plan and its scope and breadth becomes known, there will be such a groundswell demand that justice be served that even those that were on the fringe will shrink back in disgust, wondering how they ever let themselves get so close to colluding with the scheme.

"Don't worry about how this will all play out. All you need to know is that I am taking action and this will not be reversed. This is happening now and you can pray into this to give it more strength."

I looked at the LORD sitting there, His two-edged sword in His right hand. Jesus acknowledged this.

"Yes, My sword is in My right hand. My New Day is here, and those who have opposed it are paying the price. The bricks are caving in and the tower is falling!"

~SIX~

The Winds of Change

And when He brought His supreme Son into the world, God said,

"Let all of God's angels worship Him."

Regarding the angels, He says,

"He sends His angels like the winds, His servants like flames of fire."

But to the Son He says,

"Your throne, O God, endures forever and ever. You rule with a scepter of justice"

Hebrews 1:6-8

The Winds of Change June 3/2020

As soon as I sat down in my quiet place, I knew that Jesus was waiting for me. I began to focus in on where I thought He was sitting when His voice broke in saying, "Big change coming, Greg."

I hesitated at this news. "Good or bad?" I asked.

"Good," came the answer.

Now I could see that He was sitting and holding His harp again. As I rested in His presence, I began to think about the strong winds that woke us up in the middle of the night, and were now moving the trees about in my yard as I watched.

"Winds of Change, Greg," Jesus commented, looking directly into my eyes.

"LORD, I ask you to release your angels of change," I felt prompted to pray. "LORD, what is this wind all about?"

Jesus replied, "It is blowing away the chaff. Without these winds, it would be impossible to separate the wheat from the weeds (tares)."

Tare – an injurious weed resembling wheat when young.
Oxford Dictionary

Winds of Change – forces that have the power to change things—used generally to mean change is going to happen. Merriam-Webster

Course Correction July 2/2020

"Let's talk about My Church, Greg," Jesus' voice broke in. "Why do you think I have allowed a pause or re-set?"

"We weren't quite aligned with what you were wanting to do," I speculated.

"And how far do you have to be off to be off track?"

"One degree."

"The longer you travel on the wrong trajectory, the farther off course you get," He said.

"LORD, how does this relate to the current (Covid-19) situation?" I asked.

"I am allowing My Church a time for course correction. Many see this as a loss of momentum when in actuality it is more a drastic change of direction than most realize. You are in the midst of that now. This new direction that I am calling you to will allow you to gain momentum back *and more*. The Winds of Change have shifted and are blowing in a new direction. They are strong and you must let the sails out and allow them to carry you as I have intended. I have a new destination for My Church and it is not far off. Many are trying to (row, tack, sail) against these winds, but they will soon get weary and allow themselves to be carried where I desire to take them.

"Was Noah concerned with where the waters were taking Him? Though he had no idea of where or when he and his family would get off the boat, he trusted Me completely. You are getting anxious for the fall and making decisions around the church construction. Don't you see that I have made this situation to be like Noah's? I have 'shut you in' to the current on-line service delivery so that you wouldn't try to move in any other direction than the one that I have carried you on. The fact that you have had no choice has been My gift to you!

"During his time on the boat, Noah focused on tending to His family and the animals under his care. What was going on outside the ark he had no control over, so he left it to Me. Only when he sensed the waters were receding did he send the birds out to search for signs of dry ground."

Change is Necessary September 2/2020

As I looked at Jesus' chair, the sun was casting a shadow of a branch that was moving in the wind.

"Why is change so threatening, Greg?"

"I guess it is because it takes us away from what is comfortable and what we are used to," I responded.

"And how many changes in your life have brought about negative effects?" Jesus went on.

"Not many"

"Can you think of any?"

"No, I can't." This came after a long pause as I considered this. "Even the ones that I thought were negative were just hard seasons, but produced good fruit later on."

"Exactly. There is stress, anxiety and even division occurring as people realize that change is coming—is here. Think about moving you and your wife's parents out of their homes. Minor things were changed as the years went by, but by and large, things stayed the same. But when it came time to move, it was understood that a wholesale change was coming. Even the smallest, most out-of-the-way rooms needed to be examined and cleaned out. Every corner of the home had to be inspected and cleansed.

"This is how it has to be if I am to really move among My people. My glory and My presence are too heavy to be carried by anyone who has not completed some significant house cleaning *and* is determined to keep it that way. The devil uses the world and its systems to pollute the believer's walk with Me. This has been happening for a long time, so that living with this pollution becomes normal instead of seeing it as toxic. It accumulates over time like the growing number of items in a home.

"The change that is here exposes all things—good and bad. It is blowing away that which destroys and deceives, yet is drawing in new habits, ideas and protocols that will help stamp out the toxic things of the world. You have already witnessed this in a decreased desire to follow sports and an increase in attentiveness to Me and My ways. All of this without meeting together in-person.

"More importantly, the change that I bring is ushering in a New Day of fullness and completion. Time is now short. My Church must become all that I have willed her to be. So, change is necessary.

"Think about it—even with all the true expressions of My Church in your city, was the area changing *for good?* Apart from a drastic disruption, would your habits and protocols have changed in a deep and complete way? Could something so profound as My Church being kept from meeting in-person happen without My permission? Of course not!

"Think about Job. Did he have more or less reverence for Me after I allowed Satan to act out for a time? I restored everything to Job and really doubled it in the end. Would he say that the change (however long it seemed) was negative?

"In the days and weeks ahead, I will be speaking this same message to others around you. You will no longer feel like you are an island, and there will be a synergy that grows as you all become aware of how I am working in, around and through you. This will only be the beginning, but you will be truly amazed in the unity and strength of the faith and hope that I am building in the Body.

"There *is* a New Day coming, and it is close at hand. Believe Me!"

Experiencing the Winds of Change August 30/2020

"You are experiencing the Winds of Change, Greg."

"How so?" I asked.

"Can you feel the shift taking place in your soul? Would you want to go back to where you were (relationally with Me) last summer? Has there been an increase in reception and openness to Me that is tangible and real?"

I just sat there quietly with this.

Jesus continued, "Is there anyone these winds are *not* blowing over? Does everyone have the chance to receive whatever I send in these winds of change? Of course they do, but one must be willing and open to not only raise their spiritual sails, but allow Me to move them in the direction and to the place that I intend.

"This is the time for introspection; an honest inventory of the heart. The hidden places must be given over to Me just as the bigger rooms of the soul are. I see all anyway, but it is in righteousness and purity that you achieve greater heights. The winds are changing the landscape—both in the natural and the spiritual. Change is coming—must come—but everything depends on what you do with it."

I looked at Jesus in His chair and could see him holding a long, skinny accordion.

"Music is made as the wind inside moves in and out. This is what is happening in this season. The Winds of Change not only blow things away, they also *draw in* other (good) things in the vacuum. This is changing the landscape literally and figuratively, creating new and different ways of thinking. This is key to bringing true alignment to My Church. Pray for new revelation, new methods and new tracks to run on. All of this must be powered by My Spirit.

"Embrace the chance to change! It will bring great joy in the time ahead. Yes, Greg, embrace the Winds of Change!"

An Abrupt Change September 6/2020

I heard Jesus' voice tell me to write everything He was about to say.

"I am coming in a way that is unlike any way you have experienced Me before. You have no frame of reference for this; it will be outside of your 'box'.

"There must be an abruptness to My coming in order to break through the current mindset of My Church. Some are like a child who continues to look back while being tugged along by a parent. Instead of looking ahead to where they might be led to—and the good things in store for them—they look back at what was. If 'what was' seemed so good, then why wasn't it transforming the earth and impacting it in a significant way? Why does My Church look weak and powerless to those who are prideful and perishing? Why are many who are in the Church look like those who don't know Me at all?

"I tell you that there is an *abrupt change* (Yes, underline that!) coming that is going to surprise and shock many who think they know Me. 'The fear of the Lord is the beginning of wisdom' and My Church will be a place where wisdom is found. Then it will become obvious how much folly there is in following the world.

"You feel sheltered in here (the studio) because you have already begun to come to Me for shelter, for wisdom and direction. I will never fail to lead you on the right path if you come humbly and honestly to Me looking for the way to go. This is the secret to working in obedience, and this is what I am calling My Church to.

"This abrupt change will bring about a true realization of who I am. I will no longer seem like some distant deity who asks to be worshipped from afar. I am coming to reveal Myself as a God who loves My people in an up-close and personal way. Then those who have ignored My ways and My statutes will have a choice to make!

"Again, I say to you, pray for and encourage others—and soon many will encourage you with similar words. For the Spirit of the LORD is coming upon the earth in greater glory and the earth shall not be able to contain all that I am about to bring forth! Shalom!"

Change and Transformation October 7/2021

"Let's talk more about signs and wonders. Remember the Pharisees asked to see signs and wonders too," Jesus commented.

"LORD, I asked because I don't see the Church walking in power," I lamented.

"Greg, when did My disciples really begin to walk in this?"

"They discovered this when You sent the twelve out and the seventy—but Pentecost really ignited this."

"So, what happened?" Jesus prodded.

"They announced that your Kingdom had come and *believed it.* Even after your death and resurrection they began to understand with greater clarity that your Kingdom was to be advanced *through them!* They were to be the conduits of your grace, mercy and love to a lost world. They not only carried the fires of *faith*, but also *belief* in the mission you had given them and the *power* to fulfill it," I replied.

"So, do you see why so many are called to be still in this season? Why so many programs have been interrupted? Everything must be reset to the things that matter. Signs and wonders do not bring people closer to Me; mercy, grace and love do. That is why all healing and deliverance must be linked to My Kingdom and the revolution that it brings with it. The Kingdom's power is in its selflessness: Giving, not taking; healing, not inflicting; forgiving, not accusing; loving and not hating. When My Church really gets a hold of this—when this truly rests in the hearts of My people—change will break forth.

"The times you are living in now are necessary for this transformation. This is the main ingredient for the change that is coming—is here! Yes, you will see signs and wonders, but only when you understand the heart of the mission of My Church in this day. Once this happens, My Bride will break forth in great power and influence. This is the alignment that I have been waiting for and calling forward.

"This all sounds encrypted now, but shortly you will fully understand all that I have said to you, not only today, but over the past weeks as well. My glory is breaking forth and cannot be stopped. My Church is transforming because I've willed it to be so long ago. Now is the time for her to shine! Be encouraged by this and encourage others!"

A Call to Night Prayer October 12/2020

I asked Jesus what was on His heart to talk about. He reminded Me that I hadn't yet opened the Bible. Jesus directed me to Psalm 134.

> Oh, praise the LORD, all you servants of the LORD, you who serve at night in the house of the LORD.
> Lift your hands toward the sanctuary, and praise the LORD.

> May the LORD, who made heaven and earth, bless you from Jerusalem.

"Greg, you have to be willing to respond to My call, night or day, in this season. I have many, many intercessors who are spending the night with Me praying back to Me all that is necessary for the coming move to take place. When I invite you to join Me out of the comfort of your sleep, I am offering you something better!

"You are already remembering the last time I offered this to you, without you responding. There is no condemnation in this. I am however calling you to more in this season, not only for the sake of your nation, but I am offering a better way forward for you as well. I promise you that answering My call in this way will benefit you, your family and so many others around you to a very great degree.

"You have been called to pray and lift your hands in the studio towards the sanctuary where I have called you to worship Me. This is biblical and directs the righteous prayers in that direction for your benefit and My glory. Until I call you inside the temple, I call you to do this as much as you feel called to. There is a war on and it will only be won if My saints respond to My call. There is a growing number in these ranks and many are now understanding not only the call, but their part to play in all of this."

Waiting for Change October 17/2020

"Jesus, I have just read through the last five days of this journal. Help me to stay in tune with you." I had returned His chair from the studio and back into the study to help with my focusing on His presence. I noticed that He was there and it took a while for Jesus to speak.

"This morning, let's talk about waiting. Why is waiting both difficult, yet important?" He asked.

"I guess we naturally want to see what we are waiting for come to pass. Our expectation to see that 'thing' come to fruition can make waiting difficult…"

Jesus sat quietly in the silence for a moment. "Why do you think I have allowed such an upheaval of life in this season?"

I sat there, thinking through an answer to this. "LORD, you have said over and over again that you are bringing down enemy strongholds and re-aligning your Church to Your ways."

"So why doesn't this just happen instantly?" He again questioned me.

"I suppose that there is power and strength that comes from yearning for the transformation to happen," I responded. "That in the journey there is a realization that change *needs* to happen, then an acceptance that it is happening and an understanding that you can't go back to the way things were. Once that happens, a desire to see and experience the new destination or result is birthed. I sense that so much happens in the waiting… so much hidden formation that is built upon even more formation as time goes by…"

"And you can either embrace the waiting or rail against it," Jesus added. "One builds you up while the other tightens the chains of bondage even further. I am a good God! If I am having you wait, it is because I have something much better in store. And this certainly pertains to the season you are in right now!

"Greg, the formation of faith that is forming in the Body is *the* necessary ingredient in the coming of My glory to the degree that I desire it to come over the earth. 'Without faith it is impossible to please God' and My glory and presence can rest on no other. Therefore, continue to allow Me to transform you as you wait. Encourage others to be transformed in the waiting as well. I tell you that it will be well worth it!"

Necessary Winds December 20/2020

"The Winds of Change, Greg," Jesus whispered.

This was in response to remembering how the wind had come up in a strong way after early morning prayer yesterday and watching as the wind increased this morning, forecasted to reach 70 kmh today. As I sat looking at Jesus, I saw Him sitting with His right arm out. The phrase, "God's mighty, outstretched arm," came immediately to mind. At this, the LORD spoke.

"What have I taught you about the wind?" He prompted.

"Often your angels move in the wind, especially when there are many of them," I answered.

"And what am I moving against now?"

"I believe you are moving against injustice, corruption and the evil agenda of the wicked one. But I would also add that you are addressing unbelief in your Church," I added. As I looked up from writing this down, I could see that He was now sitting casually, with His arms at His side.

"Yes, all of this is happening and more, as you are about to see. I am the same yesterday, today and forever, and I do not change. But how I am perceived and believed in by mankind does change. That is why the winds are necessary. As I have told you, they are needed to sweep away all that is ungodly and unrighteous, so that the new foundation that I am preparing would be free from corrupt and toxic hubris.

"My angels are purging the land, the people and the institutions that govern them. Nothing will be left untouched. The Winds of Change must sweep into every corner, if what I will to transpire in the coming transformation is to come to pass.

"I *am* growing the faith of My people! Without this there would be nothing for My glory and presence to rest on. Yes, Gabriel was astounded at Zechariah's lack of faith in Me and the message sent, but he (the angel) had been in My presence. How good it will be for those who trust in what I am saying right now *without seeing!* How much will their faith be bolstered when I break forth the New Day and everything that I have spoken about comes to pass! How freely will My Spirit be able to move in such an atmosphere of pure and true faith! This is being laid down right now and it will be a glorious thing!"

Winds of Change and Healing January 19/2021

"LORD, I thank You for being so benevolent with Your time with me. As long as I am willing to 'stay' with You, you are willing to stay with me."

"Greg, this is only the beginning. As long as you are willing, we will converse like this for all time and beyond (when you get to the eternal home that I have for you)."

Jesus continued on, "You are concerned about the high winds that are forecasted for your region today. Don't be. It is coming as a sign to those who have yet to believe that My presence is on its way. The Winds of Change are here and all things that are about to be flipped upside down! Any time now you will see this fully transition into the natural realm, and as it does be prepared to be amazed! You (and the others who have been sitting with Me) will understand these things as they happen and for what they are. The domino pieces will begin to fall—perfectly orchestrated—like I have been telling you for months and without effort or striving on anyone's part, the Great Reversal will be underway."

"But what do the Winds of Change have to do with all of this?" I inquired.

"Do you still not get this? My angel armies move in the winds when the transition occurs between the heavenly and earthly realms. Their entry into the natural causes the wind to move and atmospheric changes to occur. The sheer numbers of their movement will cause strong winds in your area, but have been causing major wind calamities south of the border over the last week. These are all signs of the movement and change that is taking place on the earth right now. Righteousness is being restored!

"Greg, do not look at the timelines made by man, but look for the signs that My Father gives you all. Only He knows the time and the hour for such things. Keep your eyes on Me and do not look to any news sources as they simply cannot understand what our Father is doing in the moment, and neither will you if you look away from Me. Stay sheltered in Me by remaining humble, prayerful and full of faith. Then you will be strategically postured to not only see what our Father is doing, but be used by Him to give encouragement, clarity and visions as the storm stops and the New Day is born."

The LORD began to speak, but I began to lose my faith in what He was saying. Jesus commanded me to engage by telling me to write the following down.

"Watch as the numbers drop in British Columbia and Alberta first. This will move eastward and will be an unprecedented occurrence. Yes, I use that word—*unprecedented*—to stand truly against the great deception that has occurred and that has been mis-used repeatedly!

My presence is about to sweep through the hospitals and the I.C.U.'s especially, causing great confusion in the medical community as patients who were deathly ill one minute, are perfectly fine the next. This will be compounded greatly by top-down, political pressure to keep this news quiet—but this will prove to be impossible!

"This move of healing, from west to east, will precede the wave of renewal that is about to follow the same path! This is glorious new and it is all about to break forth over you shortly. Keep the faith! Be encouraged!"

~*SEVEN*~

Into the Storm

Oh, that I had wings like a dove; then I would fly away and rest! I would fly far away to the quiet of the wilderness.

Interlude

How quickly I would escape—far from this wild storm of hatred. Confuse them, Lord, and frustrate their plans, for I see violence and conflict in the city.

Psalm 55:6-9

The Prince of North America July 27/2018

I waited on the LORD and my mind was adrift. Finally, His voice broke in asking, "Where am I in the house this morning?"

"You are on the back deck," I responded.

"And who have I brought with me?" He prompted, sharpening my faith vision.

"That same Prince of North America you brought with you a couple of summers ago." Jesus was sitting in the same place and this prince with Him was standing still and obedient beside Him, just as I had seen in a similar vision before, even though the prince was a representative of a dark power or principality.

"Has anything changed?" Jesus asked.

I looked and the prince was still standing there and holding on to a large scythe with both hands, as he had a year or so before. The intent was that he would be released in the future to do great damage.

To this Jesus added, "I told you that you would have heightened discernment and I meant it! This is coming so prepare for it."

A Storm of Fear August 19/2020

I spent some time finishing the book on revival that I was reading, but concerns regarding a family member dominated my thoughts.

"Greg, don't be afraid. I am here," Jesus voice broke in.

"LORD, why am I feeling fear this morning?" I asked.

"Just as the storm last night steered mostly away from your home, you still felt the wind and a few drops. Similarly, as the Storm of Fear that I talked about draws closer, you and your family will only experience a small bit, but it is important for you to be able to empathize with others feeling the full brunt of it.

"The unfortunate thing is that this fear will be mostly unmerited—the real danger will have mostly passed over, but the *perceived* danger will fuel the storm. Much of this is centered around making decisions for others, especially the children in relation to school, but there will be other stressors as well. Do not despair and do not succumb to the power of the storm! For as quickly as it comes upon you (and your region) it will be over just as soon. Then you will see and experience the blue sky and the peace that settles over you all. This is a necessary thing to allow greater numbers of My followers (and those who have become seekers during this time) to realize and understand what I am doing—that I am actually pursuing My Church in this hour.

"My plans were set in motion before I started time and they are fully underway. Just as a woman in labor cannot return to the state she was in before the labor commenced but must push through the pain—so must My Church push through this experience. And just as there is joy and awe of My creative powers in every birth, so will it be as this New Day is realized for what it is.

"I will not remove this gift of accelerated ability and ease to come to Me—it will be available to My Church from this point on. There will be no excuse for those not in step with Me, for the veil between you and I is extremely thin now.

> Come to Me, all of you who are weary and carry heavy burdens, and I will give you rest. Matthew 11:28

A Membrane is Punctured August 25/2020

"What's on your heart today, LORD?" I asked. I usually look for Him with my eyes open, but decided to close them to get a picture of what might be important for our conversation that day. I could see that He was sitting and in His hand was a lance or pointed object. Jesus reached out in front of Him, as if to puncture or perforate some kind of membrane. This was very flexible, like latex, but I knew the lance was about to burst through. I asked Him what this was, and as I did, I could tell that if Jesus pushed even a slight bit more, this delicate barrier would be breached. His eyes looked directly into mine as He paused and held perfectly still.

"What I am about to perforate will cause an opening that allows both good and evil to flow freely in two directions. This must happen," Jesus continued, "if we are to get to the blue sky that I spoke of earlier. Gird yourself in righteousness and tell others to do the same, as while the 'air is being let out' there will be turbulence and the air of disorder. But like a balloon that has been punctured, this will last a very, very short time. Then there will be no wind left to oppose Me.

"You have been given this word to calm and reassure others in the moment—and that is all that it will be—a moment. Then you will see and experience the change that I am bringing *over* you (My Church) and the good things that I am bringing *to* you. Yes, again I say to you:

> No eye has seen, no hear has heard and no mind has imagined what God has prepared for those who love Him. 1 Corinthians 2:9

"Hold fast to Me and trust in all that I have said by faith. I am building My Church and surely the gates of hell will not prevail against it. Yes, and by 'gates' I mean the strongholds that Satan's forces currently inhabit and work from in the cultures around you. These are coming down and soon My Church will understand how to partner with Me to fulfill this.

"Sit with Me, encourage others to sit with Me, and see what I do as My people… watch, wait and wonder!"

About This Fall August 27/2020

"Greg. Let's talk about this fall."

"What do we need to know, LORD?" I responded.

"First, things aren't going to be the way you think they will be. There is a "twist" coming that will throw many off. This will be unexpected and will greatly affect leaders in many areas. This is why you must remain grounded in righteousness and faith. Then you will withstand the turbulence of what is ahead.

"Secondly (I looked over at Jesus and He was holding up two fingers) My Church is entering a new phase. Those who have been striving to return things "to the way they used to be" will fall back (not away) much as a runner in a race who simply loses energy as compared to the front runners. I have spared you (the church that I attend) from this by positioning the construction in this time period. You (Greg) get frustrated by the rain that continues to come over and delay the building of the parking lot, but I tell you I have you on a divine calendar so that you can be one of My frontrunners in all that I am doing. I will not let go of those that fall back, but for their own good they must let go of yesterday's manna in order to embrace the new.

"Thirdly, (again showing me three fingers) those that patiently await the transformation that is coming to My Church will be richly rewarded. There is no shortcut here; waiting on Me is NOT optional! Those that strive, plot and plan in their own strength will struggle like the disciples did in their boat during the storm. I was prepared to walk by them if they didn't give up relying on their own strength and call out to Me. This must be the picture of My Church in this season. You must see Me as the Prince of Peace and come to Me again and again for shelter.

"These three things—the disorientation, the new phase and the coming transformation—are all necessary for My Church to be all that she needs to be in the coming days. I will not leave you nor forsake you, and I will demonstrate to all My sovereign power as I awaken My Bride. Again, I say: Wait, watch and wonder!"

More About This Fall August 29/2020

I looked for Jesus in His chair and soon heard Him say, "Greg, I told you that I would meet you every morning, if you are willing."

"I am willing Jesus! What's on your heart?"

"Let's talk more about the fall. You are fearful after reading over our conversation from the other day. I tell you, don't be! All those who come to Me and shelter under My wing will be completely and totally protected from all that is ahead. You cannot fully understand everything that I am doing in these days, and that's ok. It may sound like a simple, contrite answer but it is important to stay close to Me, whether you feel like you are connecting with Me or not.

"The storm that is coming is going to whip up all kinds of worldly hubris that—if you listen to it—will sadly deceive many. The world cannot see or understand what I am doing in this hour, but My Church can! This must be seen through the eyes of faith, paired with walking in right-standing with Me. *Then*, you will be able to see the blue sky on the other side of all of this, and it will bring great hope!

"For I am moving in such a way as to disarm and dismantle many of the strongholds that the enemy of My Church has held for so long. It is only by allowing this storm to blow through that this can happen. This is why it is important for My leaders to be aware of this and not focused on trying to return things to the way they were—for they (the old ways) are being overturned. Instead, continue to teach and direct My people to come to Me for shelter. It is the only place of peace when all else seems like it is being uprooted!

"Again, I say that this (storm/season) will blow over suddenly/quickly. But while this is over you it will seem to have stalled and not be moving. Have faith! Be strong! Hold on to the hope that I have given you, for it (this hope) is the light in the darkness! I tell you, there is a great awakening about to take place! My peace I leave with you."

Orienting Through the Storm September 10/2020

"Let's talk about orientation," Jesus introduced. "To have orientation you need to have the right focus. If you have the wrong focus at the right time, things will seem skewed. And if you have the right focus but the wrong timing, nothing will seem to click. But… if you have the right focus at the right time…"

"How do we get focused on what *You* want us to be focused on?" I interjected.

"You are already doing this. The first step is to admit things have changed… because they have! You must embrace the New Day and all that comes with it. Otherwise, you will miss everything that I have for you and My Church in this season."

As He said this, I sensed the smile on His face and the idea that there was no way we were going to miss what he was doing.

Jesus continued, "You are thinking about Me walking on the water through the storm again. While I said that I had intended to walk by them (the disciples struggling in the boat) I positioned Myself so that they could not miss Me as I approached. The disorientation came from their not fully knowing Me. If they did, they would not have said that I was a ghost and Peter would have been able to confidently stand with Me on the waves!

"That's what storms do; they rock the confidence of the things we know and have trusted in before. You begin to think way too much about the storm and the wind, and way too little about the One who created it all."

"LORD, why did you intend to pass them by?" I asked.

"There had to be a convergence of the false reality with the real. Their disorientation was in the reality that they were living in, and not the one that was actually approaching. If they had been oriented to the true reality, they could have all got out of the boat and walked with Me to the other side. Instead, they chose to pull at the oars for hours, trusting in their own strength and focusing only on the storm."

"How do we learn from this for the time ahead?"

"Now is the time to come to Me for shelter. Now is the time to draw close to Me, and not the world and what it is telling you. As you do this, you will find a new orientation that will match the time that you are living in. Then those who are cheering you on from heaven will stand and rejoice at your obedience and character!

"There are amazing days ahead for you. Keep your orientation on Me and what I am doing. Then I will bring a new orientation to a very disoriented world!

"Watch and see, Greg. Watch and see."

A Bedrock of Faith September 17/2020

"What is on your heart, Jesus?" I inquired.

"Why are you so concerned about what transpires this fall?" He answered. "Do you not think that I have plans to look after you all?

"Yes, this fall is not going to look like any in the past, but neither are the times following it. There is a bedrock of faith that is being built in My Church (that's you!) that will be unshakeable moving forward. You read about this every time that you open up one of Paul's letters in the New Testament. Did he avoid adversity? No, it strengthened him and his trust in Me.

"As soon as you take your eyes off Me and dwell on the world's problems, you will be deflated. The deceptive spirits are ruling the day right now, but this will be for only a short time. Satan always overplays his hand and there is a time of revelation coming.

"'But for you who fear My name…' yes, there is a time of joyful celebration coming that no darkness can conceal or hide. This is coming suddenly/quickly and will catch many by surprise, even some in My Church. But you will not be caught this way; you (along with others) will make sure of this, as this is part of your assignment and how I have made you.

"All of this is coming much sooner than you think. You have seen My generals and My army at the ready—on standby to move instantly on My command! Yes, you are sensing my eagerness to bring forth all that I have promised My prophets that I would bring forth, and I will delay no further.

"You were given the privilege of seeing My timeline into this New Day. It has already begun, though there is a lag in its transitioning to the physical. This New Day brings with it the new realities that I have placed in it. Therefore, as it unfolds, you are about to see Me in a much different light, because I will not be as veiled as I used to be to you all. This will cause some to stumble, not because they don't see Me, but because their former idea or understanding of who I am was/is totally skewed. The new, authentic reality will be too much to take in; their oil in their lamps was low to non-existent. Without the help of the Holy Spirit, no one will be able to understand or comprehend Me in this new state. But there will be many who rebound from this because My grace and mercy will be poured out in even greater measure than it has ever been poured out before.

"Greg, don't fear the fall. Deception and unbelief rule for only a short time. Instead, anticipate with great hope and expectation the dawning of this New Day."

Prayer to the LORD October 1/2020

This morning I found myself writing out a prayer of surrender to Him:

"LORD, forgive me for getting into the pattern of 'have to'. I know the pattern that you want for all of us is 'desire to' when it comes to meeting and spending time with you. Father, like everyone else, I have been stripped of those things (many that are false) from where I find my identity. But I need to let this sink in: My identity comes from my relationship with You and *You alone!*

"Perhaps this is the greatest crisis that is going on in and around me right now. The indicators and measures from where I (falsely) gained my value have been taken away. Rowing in the storm is useless! Unless I see You for who you really are, I am simply going to be bounced around and tossed about on the murky waters of deception, no closer to shore than I was weeks ago soon after embarking on this journey.

"But you God never change. You have made yourself more available to me than ever before and for the most part, I have taken you up on your offer to step in. You are inviting me to not only lean into the promises that you have spoken over me (us) but to trust that what you have said is the *real* truth. For if it has come from You, it can be no other.

"I have no plan B. You have made it this way—with my life, my family and my church community. I must let go of everything that is false and that points me back to the old identity."

> I focus on one thing: Forgetting the past and looking for what lies ahead, I press on to reach the end of the race and receive the heavenly prize for which God, through Christ Jesus, is calling us. Philippians 3:13, 14

"We are in the middle of the lake and in a storm," I continued to pray. "If we focus on the storm, we will succumb to it. But if we focus on Jesus, who He really is and who we are in Him, then we will not only flourish, but we will also be carried by Him through what is left of it. He can do this! He walked on water, invited Peter to do the same, calmed the storm and instantly transported them all to the other side of the lake. (John 6:21)

"It is interesting that once the disciples truly saw who it was, they were *eager* to let Jesus into the boat. And maybe this is the real reason I must let go of my false ideas of who I am: I must make room so that Jesus can come aboard. As soon as the disciples did this, the storm was no longer the reality and they found themselves at their destination."

No Ordinary Fall October 9/2020

> All Scripture is inspired by God and is useful to teach us what is true and to make us realize what is wrong in our lives. It corrects us when we are wrong and teaches us to do what is right. God uses it to prepare and equip His people to do every good work. 2 Timothy 3:16, 17

As I studied the passage above, Jesus voice came through the silence into the quiet of my mind.

"Greg, do not get tired of reading and studying My Word. It is bottomless in depth so that humanly speaking—you can never exhaust the truth that is there. It will bring life when you feel things begin to whither, just as you look out the window and see things dying. My words bring life, like the rejuvenation that you witness each spring.

"This is not going to be an ordinary fall. The transformation that I spoke about is already occurring though it is hard to see and pinpoint right now. This change is happening in so many areas but because righteousness and wickedness are both unbridled, the spiritual atmosphere is very convoluted and stirred. This must transpire before healing can come.

"You saw the installation of the new 'skin' they were putting on your church building as it is constructed and this represents the new wineskins that My Church will embody shortly. There is a transformation taking place that is subtle and hard to see, yet extremely significant. Ask the Holy Spirit to guard the truth that is rising up in you and My Church. For this is where the true power lies to overcome evil and live a life of righteousness that attracts others in a dark age.

"This is one of the reasons why there must be a storm; the juxtaposition of the blue sky and calm after the torrents of the storm will be unmistakable and irrefutable.

My perfect peace and glory will rest upon any true expression of My Church, and the attraction to this will be inescapable to many. There will be a great outpouring of My Spirit upon anyone seeking to live according to truth and find the Way. This will truly be the embodiment of the term 'Glory Days'.

"I have shown you this as you will soon be actively releasing the things in the *Book of Things to Come.* You can only do this in concert with the Holy Spirit. Therefore, continue to pursue purity, innocence and soaking in My Word, as I will lead you in this."

The Rage of the Storm October 15/2020

"LORD Jesus, what do you want to talk about today?"

"Funny you should ask. Let's talk about hearing My voice. While you have had an increase in your ability to hear and see what it is that I am saying, many others have experienced the opposite. This has not been because I was not there ready to converse like this, or that they truly couldn't hear. No, it has had mostly to do with the rage of the storm around My people. So much focus has been spent on trying to re-orient and recalibrate to the Winds of Change that have blown in, that without a firm grounding in what I am doing, the dust and debris from deception and the false narrative that is being presented by the media has impaired many from truly communing with Me.

"I have spoken to you about focusing on Me—coming to shelter with Me—rather than focusing on the storm. Fasting from the media and mainline news has helped you to do this. Remember that this is easier to do for those who I have hidden compared to those who are out working through all of this. Don't stop having empathy for all who are out in the storm.

"But this is all going to come to a sudden stop soon. And when it does, the silence and peace is—at first—going to be as disorienting as the storm itself was. This is when those of you who are hearing now must speak up and into what has really been happening in the Spirit over these past few months. For My voice will be clearly discoverable to *anyone* who wants to converse with Me. And this is a strategic time. New tracks of thinking and doing will be laid down at this point, and following My direction will be paramount!

"Pray for discernment! Pray for clarity! For the enemy's only recourse once the storm passes will be to use what he has always used: lies! Speak forth the truth that this New Day holds! Proclaim the glory of My coming Kingdom! Declare that I am easily found by those who earnestly seek Me! For I promise to be found.

"The days of struggling to see and hear Me are over! I am drawing near and this will be an undeniable facet of the days ahead. Rejoice in this!"

More on Jesus Walking on the Water October 16/2020

I had again spent time studying the story of Jesus walking on the water, when I decided to ask Him about why He waited most of the night before going to the disciples struggling in the boat.

"Greg, they needed to experience the darkness of the night and their inability to handle the storm on their own. I knew that they must exhaust all avenues of trying to get out of the situation that they were in by their own means and strength.

"I intended to walk by and be on the shore for them so they could see that I was waiting ahead at first light, but My compassion for them overwhelmed Me. The disorientation that came over them from previous storm experiences, traditional narratives and their fixation on the storm led them *all* to not recognize Me as I approached. Fear had blinded them to the possibility that I could be walking in their midst in the moment. Peter walked for only a short time on the water not because he had little faith that he could do this act, but because his trust that he was really seeing Me wavered.

"They all observed Me replicating the fish and the loaves—with much left over—but they were quick to lose faith in trusting that *I had sent them* into the storm! Many witnessed and believed as I provided for 5,000 families, but My chosen ones still didn't understand.

"Greg, My Church is like this right now. They don't recognize that it is I who approach them in the storm. For many, their idea of who I am and how they know Me is skewed. But I am coming, and they will be astonished at not only how I calm the storm, but also in how I bring them to shore! This storm is softening hearts everywhere in My followers and also in those who don't know Me yet. Soon many will choose to affirm and re-affirm that I am who I say I am, as My glory spreads across the earth. Greg, My Kingdom will be glorified!

"Do you remember what time it was when I first started talking to you about the timeline? It was 4:00—the fourth watch and the time I came to the disciples. This is the fulfillment of that story in the earth's timeline and I am coming in order to make many, many more disciples!

"The storm is nearly over and dawn approaches. Remember what happened on the opposite shore? People saw Me as their healer, and they told everyone to come; everyone who touched Me were healed that day!

"Greg, passing through the storm is not an option. But what awaits you on the other side is worth every bit of the waiting. Fear, chaos and violence must be displaced by faith, calm and peace. These are the conditions of My Kingdom and My glory cannot rest on anything but. In order for this transformation in My Church to occur there has to be an honest, heartfelt desire to lean on the power of the Holy Spirit, rather than human wisdom and resources. Only by fully trusting in Me for all things (including financial resources) can you be in a place to overcome the storm. At just the right time, as I see My Church aligning with Me in this way, you will see your deliverance to the other side.

"Prepare for breakthrough! Get ready for the New Day!"

Sheltering with Jesus October 18/2020

I asked Jesus, "Where are You in the room today?"

"I'm standing over you. This is significant in that I plan to hover over and provide a covering shadow over your ministry. I say 'plan to' because you are always free to move away if you choose."

"Why would I want to do that?" I responded.

"Why would anyone choose to leave such sheltering? They lose focus and their faith wanes. Lies from the world and the enemy begin to erode trust and you drift away. This is a slow fade, and that is why it is so dangerous.

"I want you to know that there is still much room to draw into Me. You can come closer and encourage others to do the same. The more shelter that you find in Me, My Word and the truth, the less chance there is of succumbing to this fade.

"It is crucial that My faithful ones draw near to Me in this hour. Now is the time to recognize Me for who I really am, and to let go all of the false notions that have kept them at arm's length. I am inviting every follower to draw in; to take shelter in My covering. It is here that you will find true rest and reprieve from the storm."

"What about those who refuse to do this?" I queried.

"Those that choose to not come out of a storm and into shelter feel the full strength of the wind and rain. The same thing is happening in the world now. Pray for a turn-around where the things of this world would be released, so that eternal things that last would be embraced. Lies and deception rule the day so that perishable things are cherished over the non-perishable and everlasting things of the Kingdom of God. That was the purpose of the shaking. A new, infallible foundation must be laid that My Kingdom can be built on.

"Draw in to Me and watch as this happens. Teach others and encourage them to do the same. Come under Me as this is the only place of real peace, security and serenity in this season."

The Increasing Storm November 13/2020

"LORD, thank you for the good gift of waking me up last night to pray. I know that you kept me asking 'How long?' in the Spirit, and in a mysterious way you answered, 'Yes, Greg'. I thank you for all that you are doing and the promise of expecting a New Day ahead!"

"Yes, Greg," Jesus answered, "it is coming and is on your very doorstep. I have a great army of intercessors around the world and the numbers of these are growing as we speak. They are turning the tide and bringing righteousness back into balance (you will understand this more in the days ahead).

"Most storms have the brunt of their fury at the beginning, as the wind and rain come hardest at the onset. This storm is different in that the enemy is powering this, and sees that things are turning against their plans.

Therefore, the intensity of chaos, anxiety and confusion is growing, and not receding. Fear in many is compounding, which will cause much strife and angst as the storm reaches its apex. Because of My great love for all people, I will cut this short. When all seems lost, I will intervene and it will be obvious that *I am*.

"Then there will be a great disorientation—greater than the confusion of the storm. This is because all that was trusted in the world system will be found wanting; the worldly idols will have fallen. In the silence after the storm many will be disheartened and their souls will ache for what was. This is when My Church must be genuine and real. Those who know Me must reach out and share the truth of the good news, caring for and serving one another.

"Know also that there will be many within My Church that will need care like this, for they only thought that they knew Me, but must now be re-introduced. But even this will be short-lived as My glory comes into place. The New Day is bringing with it, new life! It will be like the most glorious spring you have ever experienced bringing with it joy, gladness and salvation. A holy awe will be felt like never before, greater than at Pentecost, because of the magnitude of the movement.

"This is a glimpse ahead at what is coming your way. Keep your faith strong and expectation high! Encourage others and wait patiently for the transformation that is on its way!"

Seeing Through the Fog November 23/2020

"Look at the fog outside," Jesus pointed out. "How far can you see?"

"Just outside of our yard and that is about it," I answered.

"And on a clear day, how far can you see?"

"Across the valley and beyond."

Jesus got to the point. "So, what am I saying in this?"

"I guess in many ways we have a fog hanging over us that doesn't allow us to see very far ahead. We really can only plan for the next day or two because we don't know what tomorrow will bring forth," I mused.

"And yes, remember what it is like to drive in the fog. You have to slow down. You need to put your lights on. And most importantly, there are places of thick fog where it is difficult to navigate, while there are other spots where vision improves and the road almost seems normal."

Jesus continued, "This is why it has been so hard to navigate through this pandemic season. You have had days where I have allowed you to see clearly ahead, and there have been other times where your vision (and faith) have been clouded, causing discouragement and frustration. This has been universally felt, but for those like you who I have shown the blue sky of the New Day and all that comes with it, it has been increasingly frustrating to wait for this breakthrough.

"In true reality, this storm will have a very short duration. In fact, it is nearing its end as you are about to find out. My intercessory army has been praying day and night and I have not turned a deaf ear—I hear them all! And I am not slow to act (as some think) but am coming suddenly/quickly to reverse all that has fallen to the kingdom of darkness. It is not a revival that is coming, but a great restoration of My governmental authority upon the earth. Only upon this true foundation can heaven's reality be built on earth. That is why you are about to see so many strongholds around you topple—things you never thought could be torn down. When they fall, they will be replaced by those who uphold the truth of My realm and sovereignty.

"So, endure the fog for a while longer. Greg, the wait will be worth it."

Clarity in the Aftermath November 28/2020

I have been reading over my journal entries from the past few months and am simply overwhelmed! You, oh God, are too good to behold!

"Greg, remember the key that I showed you? The one that was modern, meaning it is meant for today (these times)? Well, it has been opened and the door to the New Day is wide open! Very few see this as yet, and only a small number are willing to move closer to it to check it out. But I assure you, it is open!

"I've been speaking to you so much about faith and action because when I provide these openings for My Church, she will still need to walk through them. Remember I said the most critical time is *after the storm stops*. The disorientation to the new reality is unexpected and hard to navigate. So, when the deception and lies are taken away, it is only natural as a consequence to see a lack of trust in anything, even Me.

"This is why the voice of My Hidden Ones will be so important. You (and the others) will be able to validate and confirm all that has been transpiring to bring My Kingdom forth and manifest My glory. You have been given the keys to understanding and the ability to bring clarity in the aftermath of the storm. When there seems to be no beacon, no coordinates to lock on to—My Hidden Ones will bring clarity and vision from Me.

"Then things will happen rapidly as all the evidence of what the false kingdom attempted to bring forth around the world comes fully to light. This will repel great numbers from darkness and a holy awe of Me will spread throughout the earth. This will bring forth the harvest so many of My known prophets have spoken of.

"The door to the New Day is now open. Pray that My Church would see this *and walk by faith through it.* Keep your eyes on Me. Stay away from what the world is saying right now. Encourage others to take shelter with Me. Then I will take them higher, out of the fog, so that they, too, have clarity."

Producing Faith and Trust November 30/2020

I could sense Jesus sitting as I had seen Him a few times before "soaking up" what I was praying in the Spirit. I began to think of the storm of confusion that is over our culture, and His voice broke in.

"Did I send the disciples out into the storm?" He asked me.

I had to sit with this, as I immediately wanted to say "yes". I replied, "Jesus, you sent your men to the other side of the lake, but not necessarily into the storm."

"That is correct. It wasn't My idea to oppose them with the storm. You can figure out who caused that on your own. No, I had already spent time with the Father and knew what He was prepared to do in the day ahead. The storm was a tactic to delay, disillusion and defeat My followers.

"Yet, this was a critical test. I planned to walk by them to fan their faith and empower their victory over the tempest. But their traditions, myths and focus on the storm and how it had stymied them clouded their vision of who I am, despite witnessing one of the greatest miracles (feeding the 5,000) that I brought to the earth.

"So, let's talk about this current storm. Did I send the world into it? Of course not. But I am not surprised by it because the whole universe knows what is coming on the other side of this. Like My disciples crossing the lake, mankind is crossing over to the New Day. And while there may seem to be a lull in your progress, I assure you that you are moving toward it. There is no force in the universe that can keep this from being done!

"This time, the storm *will* produce faith and trust in My followers! It will start in only a few, but that will be enough. Yes, there is extreme opposition to this now because your enemy is beginning to see the futility in his plans to use this storm to defer what is ahead. The wind and the waves that you are feeling almost daily are his last-ditch effort to delay the inevitable glorious days ahead! My disciples could not see what was in store for them as they struggled at the oars. But once the reality of who I am and My nearness settled in their hearts, they were carried immediately to shore!

"My Word only speaks to the ministry that transpired on the opposite shore the next day. It does not describe the recovery and re-orientation that was needed (and, of course, rest) so that My Father's plans could be carried out, full of healing and miracles.

"So, this is a critical piece to understand. While I have said that I am coming suddenly/quickly, it is not the immediacy that is the issue here. *It is the recovery time and re-orientation to My face.* This is the purpose of My Hidden Ones and the reason that I have you (and others) sitting on the shoreline ahead. You are to be a beacon of light, hope and direction as the boats pull in. Can you do that?"

The Apex of the Storm December 14/2020

"Yes, Greg, there is much interference in the air today. The enemy is frantic even though things seem to be going their way. There is a great 'overplay' which is about to take place, that will set in stone forever the evil intent of all that has transpired up to now. Stay away from the sources you have listened to today. Instead, study what I have told you up to now and get deep into My Word.

"The other night, I told you that victory had arrived, and it has. This is what you must hold on to. Understand that victory pertains to My presence breaking forth, not victory of one earthly institution over another, for everything on earth is about to be tested by fire! I have said that I am coming suddenly/quickly and this is about to indeed happen. Ground yourself in Me. Hang on to the truth and do not let go!

"The apex of the storm approaches, but it will be My lightening that you see and My thunder that you feel and hear. *I am* moving against the storm and there will be no doubt about who is opposing it! Pray for those who I have called to stand and not shrink back, as I have placed them all in key positions around the world, and not just in America. They are the ones who will close the trap when My confrontation stops. Yes, they will be the victors, for I desire it to be so!

"The covering veneer continues to look strong and impressive, but inside there is collapse. Key pillars that were holding up the insurgence are giving way, running for self-preservation. But I tell you that I see them, and they will not escape. Others are seeing this, key positions in all spheres, and fear is finally beginning to sweep into the enemy's camps. The overplay that happens today will tip the scales that will serve up justice.

"I am telling you this so that you will not lose heart, but just the opposite. As you watch the reversal, you will be bathed in a holy awe that can only come from Me! Then you will know that everything that I have spoken to you is true!"

God's Mind Not Changed January 7/2021

Today's verse of the day:

> God also bound Himself with an oath, so that those who received the promise could be perfectly sure that He would never change His mind. So, God has given both His promise and His oath. These two things are unchangeable because it is impossible for God to lie. Therefore, we who have fled to Him for refuge can have great confidence as we hold to the hope that lies before us. Hebrews 6:17, 18

"Greg, have I changed?" I heard Jesus ask.

"No, you are the same yesterday, today and forever."

"And do you think that anything that I have told you in the past months is untrue?" He prompted.

I answered, "Again, no, as Your Word above says that it is impossible for You to lie. Everything that You say is truth, for You are the very essence of truth."

"Then why are you wavering today? You just read over your journal where I spoke about things getting worse for a time to allow *everything* that needs to be exposed the due time to expose it. This doesn't make My words to you or anyone else that I have been speaking to untrue. Far from it!

"Listen to Me! There can be no human explanation for how things are about to be turned on their head. There can be no earthly conventions, no governmental structures, no courts of the earth that will be able to be pointed at for the Great Reversal that is about to be front and center *everywhere*. No, I will allow no such things to be seen as false saviors or worldly idols. When I act, there will be no mistaking it! It will come suddenly/quickly, with all of My sovereign power, in My perfect timing! I—the LORD—say this will be so!

"I have not changed My mind. My promises and My word to My prophets has not changed. The earth is getting desperate for a savior and soon they will all see Me as the One who has been here the whole time! This will include My Church, and those who are in a posture of humility and seeking My mercy will receive a great crown from Me. Justice is coming to My house first, as it must. Pray for those who are called by My name but refuse to prepare for My coming.

"But again, I stress that you who have come to Me for shelter from this evil storm can rest in the confidence that I am doing exactly what I have said I am doing in this hour. Hold on to the hope that I have given you as you have met Me in the secret places. Hold on to the mysteries and treasures that I have given in the form of words directly from My throne. Hold on to the evidence that is unseen and do not gaze upon the false evidence that the world presents to you. Stand firm! Stand your ground in faith as I have called you to! Trust in My character and every promise that has come out from My mouth!

"Truth and justice are about to rule the day, Greg. I know you want to ask, 'how long' but simply trust that I will not allow any of this to hold the world captive one minute longer than it takes to completely eradicate the wickedness at large. Trust Me!"

The Stage is Set January 8/2021

"LORD, so many around me cannot see the truth for what it is and are so deceived," I lamented.

"Greg, I see all of that. And as you know, I am coming to put everything in order. You know this to be true, but others are still under the fog of the evil one. In fact, most of My Church is still in the fog… but My remnant! Yes, I have a few everywhere that are continuing to stand on the promises that I have spoken to them. I have not abandoned My prophets and those who speak for Me! The attack on you who hear Me clearly and speak out what I have asked you to speak has been crushing, but here you all stand! This has happened because you have come to Me for shelter.

"The stage is now set for Me to act. I am approaching suddenly/quickly and no one will see it coming. It will be unmistakably Me. It will be in My perfect timing. And it will bring a disorientation to many (yes, even those in My Church) because of the reversal and departure from the lies people have been told and believed through multiple sources for so long. I am lifting the fog in a moment, and in the next instant there will be light, calm and no oppressive fog. The New Day will dawn and few will understand how to navigate in it at first.

"But for those who have My wisdom and foresight for such a time as this, they will have great vision and understanding. They will be needed, first in My house, to bring clarity and validation that it is indeed My presence that has come.

"My movement must be led by My people, and they must not only learn to hear Me but look to see Me as well, if they are to follow Me into all that I have for them in this decade. There will be a great desire to do this because of the Great Reversal that has transpired, for My love for the earth will be so strongly displayed, that people everywhere will be drawn to every expression that truly worships Me.

"Everything looks bleak and oppressive now. But just wait. Things are about to break!"

~EIGHT~

Fire, Faith and Purity

And why worry about your clothing? Look at the lilies of the field and how they grow. They don't work or make their clothing, yet Solomon in all his glory was not dressed as beautifully as they are. And if God cares so wonderfully for wildflowers that are here today and thrown into the fire tomorrow, He will certainly care for you. Why do you have so little faith?

Matthew 6:28-30

A Mass of New Believers January 24/2019

I was praying with the prayer team at church when the LORD's voice broke in saying, "Rulers, Dominions and Powers, Greg."

Jesus was on a large, white horse that was high-stepping right to left across my line of vision. There was a great multitude of people following Him and many were holding up what looked like signs, but resembled the banners in the time of the Roman Legion of old. This crowd following Jesus was a scattered mass, but there was a growing sense of organization as I watched it move into formation behind Him.

To this Jesus replied, "They are a mass of new believers, Greg. The reason they look undisciplined is because they are—but they are all super-charged with the zeal of those who are new to the faith."

"So why are you showing me this?" I inquired.

"It is because they are coming your way. As you learn to follow My directions and stay attentive to Me, I will be bringing more."

"What about those who are in the Body right now?"

Jesus replied, "They are under a deep transforming time and season right now."

"And what about the mass of people that are coming?" I asked again.

"You have been asking for renewal for a long time now. Well, here it comes!"

The Man in Chains February 21/2019

Three of us were praying at the church, waiting for the Holy Spirit to speak. I began to see a man who was dirty and dressed in drab clothing. He was lying on the floor, clawing and scraping to get to the door. An ankle chain was holding him back. I asked Jesus who this was.

"He is the everyday church attendee," came the answer.

As I stayed with this vision, I could see that the chain extended behind him to a larger O-ring that then split into many other chains; all were fastened to the wall. They all had names like lust, debt, hopelessness, generational sin and the like written on them. I asked Jesus about the door.

"This is the doorway to true life."

One of the prayer partners there with me asked where Jesus was in the vision when we stopped to report on what we sensed He was saying to us. I really had not looked for Him.

We went back into listening prayer and now I could see someone standing off to the right of the man, but the man wasn't looking for or perceiving his existence. I couldn't tell if this man was Jesus or an angel.

"LORD is that you?"

"Who do you think it is?" He answered.

"I believe it is you."

"That's right. And who knows exactly which link is the weakest, the one the enemy sees as his strength?"

"You do, Jesus."

"So, ask Me what will expropriate this situation."

"What will, Jesus?"

"Your prayer will!"

No Room for Unbelief March 30/2019

"If you can't find Me (in the room) does that mean I am not here?" Jesus asked.

"The answer is an obvious 'No'. You are always here willing to meet."

"Then what stops you from seeing Me?"

"Even though I have met You like this many, many times before, my heart chooses unbelief over faith," I responded.

"So, what breaks through this?"

"Praise, worship and the truth of your Word."

"Like your dog on a walk, your heart always wants to return home to the natural, where you can understand and be comfortable. Meeting and conversing with Me will take you into the supernatural, where you will have to fully trust Me to understand and find comfort. There is no room for unbelief because it quenches the Spirit and faith along with it."

I was reminded of a picture of an old glass-ball fire extinguisher that we used to have hanging in our old farmhouse. It had a chemical in it that—when broken and exposed to the air—suffocated the oxygen in the room. I knew that Jesus was bringing this illustration to my mind in response to this conversation regarding unbelief.

The Gift of a Daisy August 12/2020

This was the verse of the day:

> Come to Me with your ears wide open. Listen, and you will find life.
> Seek the LORD while you can find Him. Call on Him now while He is near. Isaiah 55:3 and 6

It had rained in the night, so I was having difficulty finding clarity in my quiet time, struggling with my sinuses. My focus was not good, but eventually I sensed Jesus standing across from me, leaning against the desk. I also knew that He had given His seat to someone else. It was a woman from my past that He had brought into our time, and she held out a small, single daisy growing in a tiny pot for me to see. I sensed the flower had meaning.

Daisy – innocence and purity; childbirth,
motherhood and new beginnings.

"This is for you," I heard a voice say, though I had no idea whether it came from Jesus or the woman. In a strange way it seemed like they both spoke as one, simultaneously. "Take care of it. Nurture it and grow it."

Instantly they were gone, leaving the little pot and plant in the room to soak up both the sun and prayer.

The Key to Something Amazing August 13/2020

After reading about revival, I got up to replenish my coffee. As I sat down in the study, I debated whether the LORD wanted to meet me at the studio or in the house. I immediately sensed Jesus sitting in His chair with a large key in His hand. It was a modern key and He held it as though He was about to insert it into a lock (or something that had been locked).

"Why are you showing me this?" I inquired.

"Greg, you are about to unlock something so wondrous, so amazing, that you will wonder at how you ever lived without it. I am holding the key and will turn it and open it at just the right time. Yet it will be your obedience (along with others) that will set this in motion."

"How will we know that this is occurring?"

"You will know by the great amount of fruit that comes with this release," Jesus answered. "I am telling you that you cannot miss what I am about to unlock and the change will be apparent when it is opened. I tell you this because you have been persistent in seeking Me and—as promised—you have not only found Me, but are partnering with Me as I reveal Myself to all the people of the earth. When My presence manifests, the attributes of heaven come with Me. That means that My sovereignty and everything that is around My throne is present when I am present. As you call on Me to come in all of My majestic fullness, everything that surrounds Me in My heavenly setting naturally falls with Me into My earthly setting. There can be no other way. Therefore, if I choose to inhabit an earthly location, then it receives all of the royal amenities and perks associated with the King.

"You don't fully understand this yet, but as you stay with this and contemplate it, you will understand it to a much greater degree and see the simplicity of it. You have been faithful with a little, so I am about to give you more. Draw in and stay close—you are about to see all that you have been hoping for these past years!"

Deliverance, Innocence and Purity August 16/2020

"Greg, anything brought before Me (confessed sin) is brought before the King of kings. You wonder how there was immediate deliverance done as the disciples went out to minister... This happened because they took My *presence* with them and the power of the Kingdom. You are not far off from experiencing this. As you carry more of My presence, My Kingdom will advance with you bringing an outpouring of miracles, signs and wonders. This transpires not because you look for these signs, but that you earnestly seek to transplant My Kingdom on earth.

"Remember the daisy we brought you? You have overlooked the innocence and purity that it represents. When My Bride walks in innocence and purity, she has all the attention of the King. What she asks for she receives—no questions asked! Satan knows this well and so his main strategy is to pollute and distort the Bride's relationship with Me. That is why there has been a strong emphasis on caring for the soul/deliverance/life change over these past months. As the remnant grows (clean and purified) so does the inherent power of My Bride. This, in turn, draws more of My Kingdom into all facets of the earth—starting with My Church. Innocence and purity are the elements that renewal and revival depends on. My Bride must desire this if she is to come to Me in all fullness. Again, you will see this shortly, and this is one of the reasons why people will drive off the street and to My churches without knowing why. The desire to come clean—pure and innocent before Me—becomes too strong to stay 'as is' in My presence.

"You (collectively) have been asking for My Kingdom to come. It has arrived. The best thing that you can do is keep short accounts with Me."

The Faith Shawl August 24/2020

As I looked for Jesus in the room, I could see that He was standing across from me, leaning against the printer cabinet (His chair was still in the studio). He seemed to hold some kind of shawl in His hands.

"I am cloaking you in this. It is meant to help cover you from the coming storm. You have been affected by a friend's phone call and how far His faith has fallen. But I tell you, *it will be restored!* He and many others like him will rise up and be mighty warriors for Me once again. These are the 'dry bones' I am bringing back to life, and there are many, many of them! They once knew Me—My righteousness and power—but the world and the evil one had fooled them into living a hollow and defeated life. But this will soon change!

"I have sent this shaking to My Church as much for these prodigals as I have for those who have remained, but have cooled off in their zeal. I am bringing the zeal back!"

"What is the essence of this cloak?" I asked.

"This cloak can be no other than faith!" He answered.

> Faith shows the reality of what we hope for; it is the evidence of things we cannot see. Hebrews 11:1

"Greg, this cloak of faith will protect you from the winds of doubt and rain of unbelief. *Then* you may stand and proclaim what is actually true to bring clarity to all that I am doing in this hour."

I sensed that this garment had a hood and I asked the LORD to pull the hood over my head to cover my mind.

Focus and Faith September 20/2020

"Jesus, what was with the large group of crows this morning?" I inquired. A group of 80-100 crows were trying to fly west at the gate to our home, but seemed to be held back by some kind of force. They were making a terrible racket, so I couldn't help but be distracted in my time with Him.

"Greg, you can ask Me anything that you want. What have I shown you about your property?"

"There is a military garrison of angels here, a spiritual gateway and highways that run through, a sound portal that attracts birds…"

"So, are you surprised when something like this arises? Have I not made crows too? Yesterday we talked about focus—that what you are focused on will directly affect your trajectory. You were sitting down to meet with Me when this (the crows) happened right outside of your window. So, what happened to your focus?

"It came off you and onto what was happening outside," I answered.

"Ah, yes," Jesus went on, "can you see the similarity to what is happening now in the world? There has been so much attention given to dealing with the virus and the social unrest, that many have lost a true focus on what I am actually doing. There is much noise and spectacle distracting My leaders from seeing all that I am up to right now.

"But this is all going to change. As quickly as the crows were there, they were gone—and so was the distraction! You have been able to sit down and comprehend what I am saying to you this morning because you are entirely focused on Me! Not only that, you have come to *expect* to meet with Me like this. This has grown your faith and trust in what you have been hearing Me speak. And I have enjoyed these times with you immensely as well!"

"Jesus, what do I need to know about today?"

"Release the day to Me, Greg. Trust Me that I will guide you into what is important and what isn't. Every day is a gift—so take each one and cherish it, no matter what the circumstances are around you. Do everything with a thankful heart, knowing that I am aware of every concern that you have."

The Faith of Children September 26/2020

"LORD, I know that it is impossible to exhaust the number of topics that we could talk about when we get together."

"Actually, we are always together, but it is when you seek Me that we really connect," He responded.

I sat with this for a while in the quiet, and then invited Jesus to introduce the topic of conversation. Immediately, I began to see a painting of Jesus and five children climbing on Him as He laughs, that hangs above our fireplace.

Jesus, knowing my thoughts, responded by saying, "That picture illustrates how each of you must come to

Me like a child. Inhibitions and pre-conceived ideas of who I am must be left behind in order to find true joy in relationship with Me. Each one in the picture is finding their own way of embracing Me that is natural for them.

"Continue to tell people that I can be found. In fact, I am positioning Myself in such a way as to have My beloved ones literally run into Me. I have said, 'Return to Me and I will return to you,' and I absolutely mean it! My desire is that anyone who once knew Me, but has drifted away, would return to Me as their first love.

"Many, many others are going to find Me as they search for truth, after all that they have depended on has been shaken to the core and proven undependable. These are the ways of the world and they are being exposed for what they are: a false hope. But I offer real hope through faith in the truth of who I am. I will stand in the open and in plain sight so that many will discover Me for who I am. They will come to Me for shelter and I will provide so much more than that!

"Joy comes in the morning, and surely there is great joy in all those who will receive and accept Me wholeheartedly. There will be such synergy and excitement in this wave of new believers, that many strongholds that survive the next few weeks will come down because of their zeal for Me! They will spearhead this movement, not My established Church, but My new, innovative, sold-out Church!

"Yes, come to Me like children. Leave everything else behind but your innocence and purity, for I am making all things new! Watch and see what the children of God do in the coming days!"

The Fire of Faith October 5/2020

> So if God has given you the ability to prophesy, speak out with as much faith as God has given you.
>
> Romans 12:6

"LORD, thank you for this encouraging word," I said after reading the verse above.

"So, Greg, have I been building your faith?"

"Yes, LORD."

"And is there a purpose in this?" Jesus prompted me further.

"Yes, LORD" I again answered.

"Greg, why is it important that faith in who I am be built up in My Church for this approaching season?"

"Faith is the 'oxygen' that you work in," I mused. "Without faith, it is impossible to please you and really work hand in hand with You. You call us to *trust* You and what You say!"

Jesus seemed pleased with this. "Ah yes, now you have it! Greg, you must trust Me by faith—believing without seeing things in the physical, for now. But for those who want to legitimately draw close to Me, I will let them see what I am doing and hear My plans in the Spirit. He (the Father) allows My people to escape the fog and begin to understand all that is unfolding in this day.

"Greg, faith is contagious and can be 'caught' by others. That is why your words and the timing that you speak them in are so important. For where there is no fire of faith burning among My people, small embers must be nurtured and given the oxygen of My Word—the truth—verses the damp hopelessness of unbelief fueled by what the world tells My people.

"When you speak prophetically, the amount of faith burning within you must be stronger than the unbelief that is coming against you in any given situation. It is *not* dependent on that which the world presents, but rather the strength of your faith (which has unlimited potential). There is no situation too great for My Church to come against when faith is burning strong like a bonfire. And it is exactly this that the enemy has attempted to lay a blanket of hopelessness over to put out what I predetermined to break forth in this season.

"Therefore, nurture the fire of your faith, Greg, like never before! Stoke it and feed it until you can stand upright and confident in all that I have shared with you. Trust Me! All that I have promised to transpire will take place and you have an intricate, important part to play in all of this. My desire is to set you free to be all you have been made to be and I will not relent!

"Stoke your fire and others will catch it from you! This is a 'Thus saith the LORD' statement!"

Purity, Innocence and Freedom October 30/2020

"Greg, start reading the next chapter in the book you are reading, and you will see what I want to talk about," Jesus directed.

Just before this, I had been thinking about a tragic story my wife had shared with me regarding a teenage girl who her women's group had been praying for. This young woman had been molested sexually at a young age and was now hearing strong voices in her head that her life was not worth living. To me the greater tragedy was that she belonged to a believing family, but their expression of the Church had renounced deliverance ministry as being a hoax and a fraud. So, this girl was enduring an "alternate therapy" instead of picking up the keys to freedom that were close at hand.

"Greg, you have never seen such freedom come upon the Church as it is about to break forth!" Jesus said, with excitement in His voice. "I brought this story forward to you so you could feel a small part of the righteous anger that I have toward what the enemy has been doing to My precious ones for a long season. You have been toiling in this kind of ministry for a long time now and have proven your heart to see this come forth. Well, you are about to see an explosion of freedom!

"Remember when you were truly freed from many of the things that had ensnared you? How alive your walk with Me became? This factor alone—the freedom that I am bringing to My Church and the communities they serve—is going to be *the* factor that effects the massive harvest of souls in the months ahead.

"I am leading you (My Church) into a greater knowledge of My plans and My ways so that this will come effortlessly to those who have reached a level of maturity in their walk that this mantle demands. Yet there will be so much of this released that My Church will once again be seen as a powerful force on the earth, bringing freedom, health and vitality. The Sun of Righteousness (right standing) is rising with healing in His wings, and the kingdom of darkness cannot stand to the holy rays. I tell you Greg, you have never even dreamed that this level of deliverance could be available, let alone used by the Church!

Jesus continued, "The power in My earthly army that is rising will not come from My established Church as much as it will come from the zeal, awe and wonder of those who have newly discovered freedom that they have found in Me! This is what will power the spiritual tsunami that will race across the earth, upsetting the path of all the religious establishments in its way. This is why there is such a call to repentance in this day. Those who humble themselves will not be caught up in strands of religious understanding, but rather will be found righteous because they have trusted in My Spirit and kept their lamps full. However, there will be many who cling to false religious ideologies that have little truth to them; that paint a false picture of who I am. This will be washed away with the wave and the currents. Pray that many in My Church would fall into a repentant posture now, in this season where I am calling My flock to shelter under My wing. Anyone seeking shelter from Me will find safety in the firm bedrock of My foundation of truth.

"There is deliverance coming to many, Greg. Yes, wait, watch and wonder!"

The Drive Belt November 3/2020

After asking Jesus what was on is heart for the day, I looked at Him sitting in the chair across from me. He was holding something in the shape of an oval. The word "belt" came to mind and I realized it was a drive belt.

"Greg, the power to drive this movement comes from unwavering faith. Full trust in Me and what I am doing now must not just be understood, but *believed.* This is a whole-hearted faith that pushes out unbelief and *expects* to see and experience more of My Kingdom and all things associated with My presence.

"Yes, I am going to make this easy as you are now going to see Me active, through the ministry work of My angels, in every aspect of your community. People both inside and outside of the Church are going to start changing as they become aware of My sovereignty, power and presence. You will see things you never thought you would see, and this will astound you!

"In your mind you have already realized that the virus is dissipating, though this is going to take some time yet to actualize in the physical. Already the atmosphere is being cleansed in such a way as to bring more righteous activity to the forefront. There is a great advancement happening as you write this and the move is on.

"Remember to follow My ways and My precepts. I will lead you and the multitudes of others into much greener pastures if you are only willing to engage and step out with Me. Do not lose heart now, just as we are about to step up to the precipice of all of this!

"Also, remember that 'My ways are not your ways, and My thoughts are not your thoughts…" so much of what is coming next may not make sense to you now, but as the days progress you will gain an understanding. Stay in My Word and stay close. Encourage others whenever you get the chance, just as I am sending others to encourage you and strengthen your faith! Be humble and gentle."

Faith and Evidence November 5/2020

"Faith, Greg. I have been talking to you about faith! What was Tracy Cooke's definition of fear? "**F**alse **E**vidence **A**ppearing **R**eal". You came under the influence of the spirit of fear yesterday because you heard just the evidence that the media wanted you to hear. Only by hearing the words of My prophets yesterday did the truth settle back into your heart so that you could have peace."

"Why am I still so easily shaken," I asked Him.

"You (and many others) are still in the process of letting the truth about what I am about to do become *real evidence* in your heart. I use the word *evidence* on purpose, as you are beginning to understand how real the courts of heaven are and how important *trusting* in the evidence that you bring before Me in the courts is. When you honestly trust by faith that something is what I have said it is, it becomes irrefutable evidence. Satan's only tactic against such evidence is to convince you to walk away from what you believe. That is why faith is so important in My Kingdom, and especially to what is coming.

Jesus went on, "Imagine the impact that this (U.S.A.) election will have on the world (and its faith in Me) as this thing turns on a dime in the last moments! I tell you My omnipotence will be front and center in every corner of the world and through every media source. Even those in the farthest, most remote outposts will feel the impact of this revelation!

"There is a great and holy awe about to come over the earth that is going to suffocate the fear that the pandemic has brought. This man-made fear will be snuffed out like dousing a fire. In its place will be a holy fear and awe of Me, newly discovered and re-discovered by many, many people.

"This is going to turn economies around and bring life to cities and communities world-wide, including yours. To direct and manage all of this are My angel armies who are on standby and at My beckon call. This is where the knowledge of My spiritual highways will come into play and the interactive relationship with My Church and My angelic guard.

"All of this waiting—the unrushed, quiet time of waiting on Me—has been shaping many in the Church to lead in the way that I am calling you to lead soon. You are part of the remnant who has whole-heartedly accepted My call to walk in the giftings and shape that I have created in you. More importantly, you are learning to set yourself aside and follow Me closely—showing a strong desire to stay in step.

"So now you can see why I am stressing to keep the faith in this hour! You must trust in all that you have heard Me speak over the past months so that you do not doubt! Your carnal self has trouble when I say that you are going to be in awe of what you soon experience, but I say again that you will be delightfully shocked at what you see Me action for you and the Church in the days ahead. There will be times when you simply cannot move forward with anything, as your gratitude and worship of Me will tip beyond the scales of anything previously experienced!

"All of this hinges on your faith and trust in who I am! So, guard your faith, nurture it and allow it to grow. Receive only truth and rebuke anything false originating from the spirit of fear. Spend time in heartfelt, Spirit-led prayer. From that place you will find the strength to encourage others and help them get over the shock, awe and glory of My sudden appearance and the impact of My presence and the true reality that comes with it. Remember the struggle that you have had these past days as you minister in the season ahead, for many will be disoriented as they transition from a false worldview, to the truth.

"Continue to come to Me for your daily bread—it will serve you well! The dreams that you used to have about coming to Me like this were to prepare your soul for such a time. Again, I say that you were made for such a time as this! Stay strong! Encourage one another! Keep the faith! For at just the right time, all of what I have spoken to you will break forth. Shalom!"

Faith as a Catapult November 16/2020

"Lord Jesus, I wait upon you, for you and you alone are worthy!" I declared.

"Greg, do you believe that I have turned the page on the virus? Can I use your faith to speak the truth into others as a catapult to damage the enemy's stronghold? Yes, I can!

"James said, 'Faith without action is dead,' and, of course, he was speaking the truth. You can have all of the faith in the world, but if you don't act on it, you lack its power. And I said, 'You are truly My disciples if you remain faithful to My teachings. And you will know the truth, and the truth will set you free.' (John 8:31, 32) Yesterday, you heard it preached that the word *truth* in Greek can also mean *reality*. So, when you are agreeing with what I have said, you are agreeing with it as being the *reality* of what the thing or situation is. This is the reason why I have been speaking to you (and others) so much about faith!" Jesus exclaimed. "So now Greg, let's put the two together: 'Faith without action is dead… and you will know the reality and the reality will set you free!' Can you see why this is so important in these times? There is a storm of deception raging over the world, including My Church. The only way to see through the storm and navigate correctly is to take action in the truth (the true reality of what is).

"You have known how vital it is to stay in step with Me, without fully understanding why. Now you know more, so pray accordingly. You are already seeing the first fruit of Spirit-led prayer in your life, the life of your family and your church. Continue to soften your heart to the things of the Spirit and desire to submit to His calling. As you do this, you will see greater works than what has already transpired. There is much yet to do, but things are turning in your favor.

"Greg, the new reality is a breath away! Continue to rest in Me and look to Me for everything! Do not strive! I have turned the first page, so watch as it unfolds. This is only the beginning. Yes, wait, watch and wonder!"

Faith Leads to Higher Ground November 18/2020

"Where are you, Jesus, this morning?" I asked, struggling for clarity.

"I am in the chair, Greg. I am just waiting for the air to clear…" I heard Him say.

I sat in the silence, thinking about some church leadership issues that had surfaced.

"As long as My Church is advancing, there will always be some incursions by the enemy along the way. You must not only expect these, but know how to handle them My way. You are correct that the Church will not return to the way it was; this has been spoken of repetitively. What *will* change however is how you manage the flock. With a thinner veil comes the ability to understand in a greater way My sovereignty, strength and holiness. My character is easily seen and even simpler to understand. But so are the standards for My followers. They must shed their old religious habits, expectations and idea of who I am and exchange it for the new manna. The old will not last nor will it bring anyone closer to Me. The new wine demands a genuine faith and there is no room for religion. Those who cling to this (religion) will find it lifeless and void of any real power.

"No, I am calling My Church to higher ground. Those who choose to elevate their walk with Me will find great gain."

> But those who trust in the LORD will find new strength.
> They will soar high on wings like eagles.
> They will run and not grow weary.
> They will walk and not faint. Isaiah 40:31

"This is what I am calling My Church to in these latter days, and she will grow exponentially! There is a day of great celebration coming that no one can stop. My glory *will be* known all over the earth, as the waters cover the sea, and you will be My witnesses to this!"

Stripped of Power December 18/2020

Last night I awoke at 3:20 a.m. I knew this because I opened my eyes enough to look at my clock. Yet, I stayed where I was and returned to sleep thinking that I should really look up the meaning of 3:20.

Once I was in my quiet time, I was reminded of the wake-up call. I first researched the meaning of 3, and then 20. On a whim, I punched in 3:20 together into the search engine and hit return. Of course, the first thing to emerge was Revelation 3:20.

> Look! I stand at the door and knock. If you hear My voice and open the door, I will come in, and will share a meal together as friends. Revelation 3:20

The meaning could not have been clearer! Jesus loves to pursue us—at all times of the day or night—with His great love for us that hungers for relationship. He is my friend and is always desiring a deeper, more intimate relationship with me, for my own good! Last night was just another example of how comfort often usurps my seeking His always-available presence.

As I prayed in the Spirit after this, I began to sing out different phrases. After a few minutes of this, I heard the LORD's voice break in saying, "Strip them!" My singing increased as I continued on like I had before. Once again, I heard His voice, except this time He declared, "You *have* stripped them."

"Who LORD?" I asked.

"You don't need to know. But they have been stripped and have lost their power," He stated.

There was a pause as we sat together in the silence.

"Greg, write this down. Today you are going to see a sign of this in your region. Don't look for it as I will be bringing it to you. Stand on your faith, for that is what we have been building up in you all of this time. It will soon reach a point where you will be able to give it as an impartation and transfer some of the overflow that you have, so that others receive some of it too. This is the bonfire that I have started from the Iona Abbey embers that are catching flame right now. Soon, anyone who comes near you will be licked by the flames of renewal. It will be the tongues of fire, joined by the evidential truth of the changing times that will bring this all forth! You (and the others that I have been preparing in this way) will be like walking torches and your faith will set whole neighborhoods ablaze in want of Me. I will this to be so, and so it will be!"

Light Exposing the Darkness January 9/2021

There have been a number of times now that I have sensed Jesus sitting across from me, His arms outstretched toward me with palms out, seemingly absorbing everything that I was praying in the Spirit. When this happens, I feel such a deep communion and connection with Him and feel like I could partner with Him to accomplish anything.

Jesus began to speak to me. "Greg, you have been declaring and decreeing that the virus disappear in your province and country. This still takes you to the very precipice of your faith and trust in Me. Don't let it! You just read through the Beatitudes and know that My gate is narrow and few go through it. This is the entryway to trusting that I can do anything in your life, even that which seems impossible to those on the broad, wide way. What have you read numerous times? 'Then your Father, who sees what is done in secret, will reward you.' Yes, My Father sees every hidden and wicked scheme. But He also takes notice of every righteous petition that has been poured out to Him behind closed doors. Do not underestimate the power that you (and many, many others) have been tapping into as you have retreated to your places of prayer. These have been battlements of great might that have demolished many strongholds held by the enemy, and continue to do so. You sit here and wonder how a simple act of raising your right arm and swirling it around in a circle as if cutting through some imaginary substance can hold any merit. But I tell you, these proclamations and actions, when prayed in agreement with Me, can bring whole earthly establishments tumbling to the ground in rubble!

"Yes, there is a tiny spark of understanding this in My Church—but it is about to grow into a raging inferno! More and more of My prayer warriors are spending this kind of time with Me—and the result is changing the world! You see so much upheaval on the earth right now because this is part of the transition. Light is exposing the darkness and everything that has loved the darkness and has hidden there now has nowhere to turn. They will quickly turn on one another, a consequence of taking that path.

"But My Righteous Ones are rising in strength and in numbers! Yes, Greg, this is something to celebrate as they will usher in My presence, and with it, My glory. It *will* cover the earth as the waters cover the seas. You can bet that I am taking away the virus! It has been used too long already as an excuse to mute My Church and incarcerate the people of the earth whom I love dearly. This has truly been the crime of the century and when it is removed (wait for it!) ... I will receive the true honor that I am due.

Very few of My prophets have understood this, but you have.

"Greg, take off your clothes of sackcloth—your days of mourning are over! Instead, raise holy hands toward the sanctuary of your God and sing and give praise for all I have done and am about to do in your midst! Yes, shout for joy as there is a great celebration coming and you will see it all unfold."

> Give thanks to the LORD, for He is good,
> His faithful love endures forever. Psalm 107:1

Faith into Action January 13/2021

"Greg, what is the evidence of your faith?" the LORD asked me.

After thinking for a minute, I responded, "I come to You every morning *expecting* to hear from You. I open my journal and date it, *expecting* you to speak truth to me; to guide and teach me more of Your ways and where You are working in the world around me."

"Yes, I do all of that. I provide evidence that I am surely at work in you. But what about *your* faith? Is the level of your faith strong enough to be put into action? Jairus showed Me his faith by coming to me, kneeling down and asking Me to come back to heal his daughter. Even with the news she had died, his faith in Me did not leave him! Likewise, the bleeding woman came and touched My garment, while the blind men testified to who I am by walking behind me through the streets and calling out to Me. This is faith put into action!

"Greg, the attack on the legitimacy of My prophetic voices has been very strategic on the part of the enemy. If My people stop coming to Me to listen and pray, and the prophetic voices that declare what I am about to do are ignored or discredited, expectation drops which in turn dissipates hope and faith."

"But LORD," I responded, "You have been so kind to me (and I believe many others) in giving us detail after detail of what is coming and how to manage it all after things turn around."

"And has this been done by accident? Or do I have a purpose in all of this? Of course, I do! This is precisely why I am about to reveal My Hidden Ones. I've been having you all look at the evidence of these past few months so that when I call you to stand on the evidence (like a court room) you will not waver. Your trust in the truth of all that I have revealed to you *will be* the reality of what has transpired, no matter what falsehoods are presented to the contrary. Yes, those days are approaching, but it will be I—Myself—that stands with you to uphold the truth. Then victory will be served and the table set. For there will be a great banquet of celebration on the other side of this that will be unmatched in history!

"You have memorized Hebrews 11:1 because it is the absolute essence of all that we have talked about this morning."

> Faith is the reality of things hoped for, the evidence of things unseen.

Jesus went on, "You have been shown the *reality* of what is coming after I take the storm away. This is what has been *hoped* for over many generations. The *evidence* has been piling up all around you both in the spiritual and the natural. They all point to a future yet *unseen*, but indeed very, very real. I am calling you to give voice to this, as I prompt you, and it is My prophetic voice's call to encourage and strengthen My Church. I also call you to overcome the opposition, take thoughts captive and step out with Me when I command this. Prepare to step out and make a difference!"

Stand Under Pressure January 17/2021

"Lord Jesus, what's on your heart today?"

"Stand under pressure, Greg," came His reply. "I am asking you to stand under pressure with your family situations, as well as the weight of what you feel going on all around you in the world right now. For in a moment—in the blink of an eye—all of this is going to change! Then you will say, 'Where has all the opposition gone? Why is there suddenly no oppression?'

"I am teaching you to stand under pressure for this is necessary training for certain circumstances that will arise in the New Day. You (and many others like you) will, at times, need to stand and not back down. You will need to lean into Me, just as you are now, in order to stand firm and gain more ground in the name of the Kingdom of God. You will discover that the trademarks of the enemy—manipulation, intimidation and control—are quite transparent in the days ahead and lack any real power when exposed like this. My Kingdom has all the power, and as long as you don't concede ground by agreeing with lies, you, others, and My Church will move forward with great effectiveness.

"Do not be intimidated! Do not be manipulated or controlled by anything other than the truth! Stand firm against all lies and deception coming at you! Then you will begin to see how very powerful you are, indeed, because you stand for the unmovable, unchangeable, eternal Kingdom of Almighty God!

"You know what My Word says and you have many, many words from Me explaining how things are about to play out in the world. Do you not think that I will take care of the much lesser issues in your family? I will do this and more!

"I have told you that there is a great celebration on your doorstep and this has not changed. The holy awe that you are about to encounter will be unlike anything you have ever witnessed. In a short time, all that you have endured will seem like a distant memory and part of you will wonder why you were so deeply affected."

The Faith of My Remnant January 20/2021

> Pride leads to disgrace, but with humility comes wisdom.
> Honesty guides good people; dishonesty destroys treacherous people. Proverbs 11:2, 3

"LORD, should I tune into the (U.S.) inauguration?"

"Greg, why would you do that," I heard Him say. "You will be able to tune into the real one soon enough. Isn't it obvious regarding what I have said to you and the authentic voices who have been spending time with Me? Why falter now? If there is anything to see from today, trust Me, you will see it many times over and from many sources.

"Look at the proverbs that you read today. Could I make it any clearer? Those who have not earned true authority cannot take it; they simply can't carry it. Wickedness cannot support a mantle that has been honestly designated to authentic leadership. This will soon become obvious!

"I am more interested in the faith of My remnant—those who have not conceded to the quickly disappearing false narrative—but those who have clung courageously to My Word and what I have been clearly saying through My true prophets. I have taken My prophets through the fire and they have proven themselves faithful! They will be honored as I am honored when the mantle of power is restored to its rightful position."

> The whole city celebrated when the godly succeed; they shout for joy when the wicked die. Proverbs 11:10

"The celebration that is coming will not be about the demise of people. It will be over the utter defeat of wickedness and the evil, evil plan that was trying to usurp all of the governments and people of the earth! When all of this is suddenly/quickly exposed and people everywhere (even those who supported those directly involved in the ruse) will jump for joy and relief as they realize what they have been saved from. This celebration will be greater than the end of any war from the past and everything will point to Me and what I have orchestrated.

"The heaviness and sense of wrong-doing that most are picking up on from the events of today will linger until I act—but act I shall! Get ready, for I am about to turn your mourning into dancing and put a song of victory on everyone's lips!

"Do not despair! Last night's wind storm should be enough for you to know that the invasion of My armies into your region is in full swing and the enemy is in retreat! To them it seems like there has been an endless supply of the troops of heaven righteously overwhelming every dark stronghold which once held down the evil strategies of wickedness. As this wind continues to blow, so too, does My mighty campaign to obliterate the camps of hell and re-instate fortresses of righteousness. This *is* happening as you write this and it *will* be seen in the natural shortly!

"Stoke the fire of your faith! It is needed, and will be needed, to spread this good news everywhere!"

~NINE~

Exposure and Light

Carefully determine what pleases the Lord. Take no part in the worthless deeds of evil and darkness; instead, expose them. It is shameful even to talk about the things that ungodly people do in secret. But their evil intentions will be exposed when the light shines on them, for the light makes everything visible.

Ephesians 5:10-14

Awaken to God's Character and Strength September 7/2020

I was tempted not to meet with Jesus today. Twice I checked the spirit(s) I was discerning, sending unbelief and blocking spirits to where Jesus would have them go. Finally, His voice broke in.

"You have an understanding of what is coming, Greg. This has taken time in the natural to unfold but you have been faithful in staying with it. This revelation of My character and My sovereignty to My Church is not that far off, as you are about to see. As My remnant awakens to this truth, more people around you will see this also.

"Greg, I see everything that is going on in the earth. Nothing gets by Me and I see all the injustice, no matter how secretive and hidden it was intended to be. As evil grows in collusion, so too, do My plans to awaken My Church. You (the Church) have everything you need to bring forth transformation. You simply must awaken to who I am and how very close I am to each of you, then you will step into the transformative power as you revere Me and understand just who I am."

The Narrow Gate September 19/2020

"What's on Your heart today," I asked Jesus.

"The things of this world are not what they seem. To you right now they seem so real and vibrant, but all of this will pass away," He introduced. "What I want you to see is what will last forever—anything to do with My Kingdom and all that I am bringing forth.

"What you *focus on* in this season is inherently important to how you (and others) will prosper. Those that authentically look for and to Me for next steps will thrive. Those that strike out on their own—even with the best intentions to honor Me—will struggle at best.

"The gateway into this new season is narrow and it must be entered following My terms. There is no room to come in self-reliance or using worldly schemes and plans. Such things will be instantly burned up in My presence and cannot stand in My glory. Instead, follow My Spirit in everything you do, everything you plan and everything you dream. Then you will be in step with My heart and for everything I long to give you all.

"My heart is for you to thrive and prosper! My glory wave was coming over the Church before Covid-19 arrived and it will not be delayed. I am readying My Bride for this. The fallout of all that has transpired because of the virus has caused great damage, but I will not stand idly by! This will only accelerate all that I had already planned. The season ahead will be the richest harvest of souls the earth has ever witnessed, and the hunger for authenticity and truth will be the fuel that drives this awakening.

Jesus continued, "As Satan's schemes and co-conspirators are revealed for what they are, there will be a vacuum of truth that enters and fills all facets of society. Then it will take great energy and determination to purposely dismiss My power, strength and sovereignty. I tell you this to confirm what others are saying. You constantly come to Me and I consider you My friend. Stay ready. Focus on Me. There are exciting, adventurous days ahead! Yes, Greg, shalom!"

Purging the Secret Places October 11/2020

"All will be laid bare, Greg. My Church needs to understand that even the darkest corners of the soul lay exposed to Me. Nothing is hidden. In the coming days there is going to be a purging of these 'secret places' personally, in communities, businesses, organizations, professional sports, governments and the like. This is a necessary step as I draw closer and is a good thing. Whether you stand before the Judgement Seat or the Great White Throne, all will be exposed and laid out in time; nothing will ever remain hidden and in the dark, for there is no darkness around Me," Jesus said.

"Only then will what I am asking (especially My Church) for in confession and repentance be recognized for the great gift that I was offering all. It will be understood but too late to action. The time is now!

> Then, if My people, who are called by My name, will humble themselves and pray and seek My face and turn from their wicked ways, I will hear from heaven and will forgive their sins and restore their land. 2 Chronicles 7:14

"The bedrock of humility is admitting one's faults and sins; gaining an understanding of how far one is from My standards. This is why I am bringing a true 'fear of the Lord' wave over My people. It will stand in stark contrast to the demonic fear that has been associated with the pandemic. No, this holy, reverent fear is the antidote to the worldly fear as it drives people under the shelter of My wing. There has been little difference between those in My Church and those who walk in the ways and the embrace of the world because there has been little to no real fear of Me and who I am. As this fall progresses, this is going to change in a profound way. Suddenly My ways and seeking Me will be the only thing that matters to many in My Church and beyond. Even the prodigals, those who once knew Me well but have drifted into worldly ways, will come running back to Me in holy awe. This awe is going to be undeniably Me, to both My Church and the unbelieving world. It will cause a great stir and there will be even more unrest. But don't lose heart, for I have overcome the world!

"Greg, do everything you can to pursue purity and right standing with Me, every day and in every waking hour. Encourage others to do the same. I am *not* idly standing by in all of this! Prepare the way!"

Roll Back the Covering October 19/2020

As I was praying in the Spirit, I became aware of one of the last phrases that I had been repeating over and over again. "Make my heart and your heart, LORD, as one." After a few moments, I became aware of a second phrase, "Not my will but Yours be done." And then came a third, "Your will be done on earth as it is in heaven…"

Jesus then began to speak to me directly. "Greg, My prayer army is learning to follow Me in the Spirit. These prayers are laser-accurate and the right thing for the right time. This is a critical period, as I am rolling back the covering that I have been showing you all of these months.

"Many things are being exposed and about to have a great light shone upon them. People's unrighteousness, even in My Church, will be exposed and brought into the light. This is happening now and it will not stop until it has reached the level that I predetermined it to stop at. If I didn't set limits with My grace and mercy over this, no one would be able to stand. My righteous fire approaches and you and all of your community would do well to stay humble and seek purity, honesty and integrity.

"There is a great era of repentance, consecration and transformation coming not only to My Church, but government, schools and all kinds of organizations. This uncovering will bring a wave of reverence as the fear of the Lord dispels demonically-positioned uncertainties that have gripped the world.

"Greg, this 'fear' exchange is going to be one of the biggest game-changers of all time. Never before in all of history has there been such a transition at so grand a scale. The difference, for those that take this offering, will be life-transforming and shift the trajectory of lives worldwide. One was slowly poisoning the thinking of people, while the other will bring clarity, understanding and purpose. It will suddenly make sense to do what is right!

"Watch as this unfolds and be amazed! You (and the others who have been pining for revival) will not believe what is going to happen, for you simply have had no frame of reference to comprehend this fully. Continue to pray in the Spirit and encourage others to seek this as well. Now is the time to *move*!"

The Live Trap October 25/2020

I looked at the empty chair in the study and immediately heard in my spirit, "Yes, Greg, I am here."

"What's on your heart to talk about today?" I asked.

"Who said I wanted to talk?" He responded.

Before I could be taken aback, Jesus dropped His gaze to something that He was holding on His knees. It was some kind of contraption that seemed like a mousetrap. It was one of those mechanical types—a live trap—that catches one, then kicks it into a holding area ready for the next one that comes in.

"Greg, My traps have been set for some time and are beginning to be set off in greater numbers. Now is the time for My light to shine into the darkest corners. This will be true for people, businesses, organizations—and yes—even My Church.

"The time has come where righteousness must win the day. If this wasn't so, the end would be pre-empted. No, you have seen the timeline. This is a New Day, and as such, it must break forth like the dawn. Just as you sit now and feel the sunlight streaming in on your face, so too, must My light shine into the farthest reaches of darkness.

"This will cause a great awakening to an acceptance and knowledge of who I really am. As you read in Ephesians—

> Their (unbeliever's) minds are full of darkness; they wander far from the life God gives because they have closed their minds against Him. Ephesians 4:18

"The light that is coming—is here—will give no one an excuse to ignore the light, for it will be everywhere! My Spirit is readily available to anyone seeking to turn from the darkness and follow Me and My ways.

"My justice also breaks forth; it comes with the light. And because of this, there is a great awakening to My holiness and complete sovereignty that will bring a wave of holy awe over My people. Even with the testimony to My presence there, many on the earth will choose to seek any form of darkness, rather than turn to and embrace the light. This is part of the great mystery of iniquity.

Now Jesus became excited. "But you, you are set to lead a great harvest! You find it hard to believe that things are changing in you and your family, but they are! As this day breaks forth, you will emerge as the natural leader that I have made you to be over all of these years. Forget the things that the world says that you need; the only thing that is important is to love staying in step with Me and My ways! This is a rhythm that you have embraced with all of your heart and have proven to Me time and time again.

"No, this is going to be different than anything you have ever done for Me before. That is why this preparation period has lasted as long as it has. This time 'under the dome' will be spoken of as the most essential process of your life! Without it, you simply would not have the capacity to carry the assignment through to completion.

"Be patient! For in just a while, there will be so much to take in that you will be overwhelmed with My goodness and all that I am bringing forth. Be encouraged. Encourage others. Guard your heart and mind. Trust in My Word and the promises that I have given you."

Revelation Coming November 17/2020

I left in the morning to take a relative to an appointment. While waiting, I read an article that had a negative effect on my faith. Once home, I decided that I needed to spend time with the LORD to get some peace.

"Why are you so easily shaken by what you heard and read this morning? Have I not spoken to you about what I plan to do? Am I not in control?" He questioned me.

"The nations (and those who think they control them) do fight and plot against Me. But all of this is in vain. The secrets that hide from mankind cannot be hidden from me and I expose who and what I want. I've told you revelation is coming in great measure and magnitude. This is partly why there will be such disorientation when the storm suddenly stops. It will be unexpected. It will have impact. It will, above all, reveal My character of justice, righteousness and love. Greg, you think the twist that I said is coming is the reversal of the election. Turning the page on Covid-19 is only the first of these!"

"LORD, why are you telling me all of this?" I asked.

"It is because you are one of My Hidden Ones. You have no platform yet, to share My thoughts to you. But soon you and many others like you will be brought forward to quelle the angst and speak truth and balance back into the world—starting with My Church.

"Continue to call forward the idea that I am coming. Encourage repentance and a desire to follow Me. Do not be disillusioned as things worsen for a short time around you. Stand strong against the deception! I am taking the virus away and you will soon know that it is so! This is the twist that no one saw coming and it will be my trump card against the schemes of the wicked. Wait, watch and wonder!"

Blow the Whistle November 20/2020

Last night I woke up at 4:55 a.m. Even though this was an hour later than the last few times, I felt God's invitation to join Him. As soon as I entered the closet, I heard the LORD's voice. "Let's do some warfare prayer. We'll do great damage to the enemy."

I began praying in the Spirit but unexpectedly changed to petitioning the LORD in English to move against the "untraceable" sources of Covid-19 that have been reportedly occurring in the Edmonton region and Alberta, along with the rest of Canada. In a mixture of praying both in the Spirit and English words, I asked for holy fire to come down upon the demonic strongholds that were creating these sources of infection and reveal them. My spirit was bearing witness that this was having an impact against these strongholds simply because I was partnering with the LORD as He requested.

But in the midst of this I suddenly thought that praying as a "lone ranger" in this was not good. Immediately I sensed the Spirit's peace over me and realized that I was on a type of spiritual "zoom call" with many others, praying and agreeing with Jesus' plans congruently and together. A great number of them were form B.C., a time zone one hour behind me and therefore my 4:00 a.m. prayer partners. This realization gave me great courage to continue praying, calling even more fire down upon these demonic strongholds and agreeing with almighty God and His plans moving forward."

"LORD, do You want to speak into this further?" I asked.

"I have explained to you that faith must connect with the true reality of things. My prophets and intercessors are growing in understanding this concept. This enlightenment has come at this time because of the willingness of My remnant to come alongside Me; to set everything else aside and truly walk with Me.

"This is the intimate relationship I cherish and long to have with My Bride. I have been willing, but for so long she has not desired to come to Me in this way. Not so anymore! This is part of the transformation that is needed to take place this fall for all of the other pieces to come into place. The intimacy factor has just increased ten-fold and this is a complete game-changer that the enemy cannot stand against. As more and more of My followers begin to ignore the distraction and choose to look for Me in a true and honest fashion, the level of faith in My Church will grow as the power of deception, lies and fear dissipates.

"Again, I tell you don't look to the world's measures to check if Covid-19 is lessening, for the ruse will be kept up for as long as possible that it is still around and potent. Despite this, it will be My Church that will 'blow the whistle' on the fact that the virus is disappearing until there is no justifiable trace of it left.

"You will understand better how this will all unfold soon but be assured that I (God) will get all the glory for this. It will be verifiably and undeniably Me! For the most part, the media will ignore this fact but My witness will spread through My people. This is the wave or surge talked about by My known prophetic voices, and what I have been saying would happen through them.

"Be patient with your brethren and remember how little of this you understood just months ago. Stay in step with Me and cultivate innocence, purity and intimacy with Me. Much is yet to be done and there will be a great harvest! My peace I leave with you!"

Not Slow to Act December 13/2020

"Jesus, you knew that My heart was heavy yesterday and the kind of day we would have," I started.

Jesus sat across from me, smiling. "Greg, you looked for comfort from the world—but you won't find it there. If you had come back to Me and sheltered under My wing, you would have gained strength to face the day. But I *am* hearing you and millions of others as they cry out to Me, and this is daily changing My Church. I am not slow to act, as some think, but I am waiting *for your sake* so that the entire plan is executed to perfection. When I act it will be with complete justice for what has transpired. How did Asaph finish the psalm I directed you to read this morning?

> Arise, O God, and defend your cause.
> Remember how these fools insult You all day long
> Don't overlook what Your enemies have said
> or their growing uproar. Psalm 74:22, 23

"I see the apparent cockiness of their position as things get overturned by the earthly courts in their favor now. This must be so to draw out many, many others who are in collusion with this evil movement. Remember, I have said that I am coming suddenly/quickly and this will happen for a reason. When I act there will be no secret place to return to, no corner to shrink back in, because My light will illuminate all!

"Greg, do not despair and do not look at what the world says for comfort, for that narrative is full of deception! The zenith approaches but you will only be able to manage if you come to Me continually for peace. For until I act, it will seem (from the outside) that despair rules the day. But take heart, for I have overcome the world!

"Like Asaph, call out to Me and I will hear you and act on your behalf. Then My Church will know Me in a whole different light and this will open the gates to My presence and My glory. Oh yes, I hear you and so many others! And I will not turn away from My people as they call out to Me—as you will soon see!"

A Righteous Anger December 26/2020

"Greg, be glad when you are unfairly persecuted and targeted, like your province has been, for it is helping to expose the darkness in higher places. If the consequences of the restrictions were not so harsh, people would go about their business and not notice. The restrictions carried over Christmas and New Year's will serve to highlight the iniquity covering the entire earth right now, and provide fuel for the righteous anger that is to follow.

This righteous anger will be felt directly from Me as I suddenly/quickly stop this scheme in its tracks, shining light on everything that hoped to remain in the darkness. All of mankind will know about the crimes committed by those who thought they were untouchable! Yes, I have a surprise for all of them! Then you will see what David wrote about Me regarding the coming harvest.

> LORD, your name is so great and powerful! People everywhere see your splendor. Your glorious majesty streams from the heavens, filling the earth with the fame of your name!
> You have built a stronghold by the songs of babies. Strength rises up with the chorus of singing children. This kind of praise has the power to shut Satan's mouth. Childlike worship will silence the madness of those who oppose you. Psalm 8:1, 2

"Greg, now you can see why the enemy has come at My people's worship with such vigor! True worship silences the enemy and all that he tries to say through his lies. Part of what is coming is a wave of faith that empowers a pure and innocent walk free from condemnation—like young children let out to play! This will usher in the New Day as the Sun of Righteousness rises with healing in His wings! Yes, you can proclaim that this is coming, because it is!

"Understand this! I have set the times and the seasons, not Satan! He will not have his way nor his conspirators with him. They are all about to be thrown down and are, at this moment, making things worse for themselves. This is all playing out completely and intentionally according to plans made long before the earth was created.

"So, fear not! Again, I say do not fear! For I am never late and everything that I have commanded will come to pass. God's decree!

"Again, I say pray for My chosen ones standing in the current strongholds held by the enemy. Pray that they would not faint in the day of adversity, but would stand like pillars holding up truth and integrity until the day that I act. For this is coming swiftly and they only need to hold out for a short time now.

"More than ever, keep your eyes on Me! I am the great Redeemer and it is only I who can remove the wickedness from the land and make all things new again! Come to Me, all who are weary and carry heavy burdens, and I will bring you rest!"

Appearing Weak December 29/2020

Jesus' voice broke in after a time waiting on Him.

"Greg, do you remember a few weeks back when that gentleman talked about President Trump? That when he acts weak, he is really in a place of strength? Why do you think that he is doing that now?"

"It seems that he (President Trump) wants everyone to think that he is getting ready to concede the election," I responded.

"And why do you think I am having him do this?" He asked again.

"Those who have worked the global agenda will gain confidence and everything associated with them will be further exposed," I answered.

"That is right," Jesus said. "In earthly terms, wickedness has raised its head on a massive scale! There has never been an uprising of evil like this in all of history. Therefore, there must be a complete vetting of all that opposes Me, as can be mustered. Every line and artery leading to the main sources of corruption must be identified and noted, so as to be dealt with in the days ahead. Just as someone stricken with cancer must be examined to expose all traces of the aggression, so too, must there be a time to allow the revelation of every source of evil that has reared its ugly head.

"Donald J. is still My man and is still president of the U.S.A. and will be! Don't be surprised if it appears that he is stepping down, as this will only serve to make him look defeated, when in actuality he holds every card to victory! Again, this may happen only to bring to light the heads of the dragon who have slithered under cover, with the intent of re-appearing once the dust has settled and the heat on them has been taken away.

"I am behind this all and it will happen on My terms and in My timing! Yes, the stakes are very high and this is why I am so involved! The whole world is being crushed by the strength of Leviathan, but I am coming to smash his heads and send him cowering in defeat! Pharaoh has dared to oppose Me and I will testify against him in front of the whole world. Yes, this will be the trial of the millennium!

"Do not believe what you hear, even from seemingly 'trusted' sources. You must trust by faith the evidence that is unseen but real, against the evidence that is seen, but unreal. I am making a path forward for the righteous as I did in the day of Moses and Joshua. What does My Word say about the wicked?

> They are like worthless chaff, scattered by the wind. They will be condemned at the time of judgement. Sinners will have no place among the godly. For the LORD watches over the path of the godly, but the path of the wicked leads to destruction. Psalm 1:4-6

"This is a time of separation, Greg. It must be completed in its due time in order for My desired result to be all that it is intended to be. Therefore, pray that everything that needs to transpire will come about as I have planned.

"Yes, prayer matters! I have received plenty from My people but more is needed to bring everything to its desired end. Encourage others and be encouraged!"

No Human Explanation January 7/2021

Today's verse of the day:

> God also bound Himself with an oath, so that those who received the promise could be perfectly sure that He would never change His mind. So, God has given both His promise and His oath. These two things are unchangeable because it is impossible for God to lie. Therefore, we who have fled to Him for refuge can have great confidence as we hold to the hope that lies before us. Hebrews 6:17, 18

"Greg, have I delayed?" the LORD asked.

"No, you are the same yesterday, today and forever."

"And do you think that anything that I have told you in the past months is untrue?" He inquired.

"Again, no, as your word above says that it is impossible for You to lie. Everything you say is true, for You are the very essence of truth," I answered.

"Then why are you wavering today?" Jesus countered. "You just read over your journal where I spoke about things getting worse for a time to allow *everything* that needs to be exposed, the due time to expose it. This doesn't make My words to you or anyone else that I have been speaking to untrue. Far from it!

"Listen to Me! There can be no human explanation for how things are about to be turned on their heads. There can be no earthly conventions, no governmental structures, no courts of the earth that will be able to be pointed at for this Great Reversal that is about to be front and center everywhere. No, I will allow no such things to be seen as false saviors or worldly idols. When I act, there will be no mistaking it! It will come suddenly/quickly, with all of My sovereign power and in My perfect timing! I—the LORD—say this will be so!

"I have NOT changed My mind! My promises and My word to My prophets has not changed. The earth is getting desperate for a savior and soon they will all see Me as the One who has been here the whole time! This will include My Church and those who are in a posture of humility and seeking My mercy will receive a great crown from Me. Justice is coming to My house first, as it must. Pray for those who are called by My Name but refuse to prepare for My coming.

"But again, I stress that you who have come to Me for shelter from this evil storm can rest in the confidence that I am doing exactly what I have said that I am doing in this hour. Hold to the hope that I have given you as you have met Me in the secret place. Hold on to the mysteries and treasures that I have given you in the form of words directly from My throne. Hold on to the evidence that is unseen and do not gaze upon the false evidence that the world presents to you. Stand firm! Stand your ground in faith as I have called you to! Trust in My character and every promise that has come out form My mouth.

"Truth and justice are about to rule the day, Greg. I know you want to ask 'how long' but simply trust that I will not allow any of this to hold the world captive one minute longer than it takes to completely eradicate the wickedness at large. Trust Me!"

Traps Closing Quickly January 16/2021

"Greg, do traps close quickly?" Jesus seemed to ask out of the blue in our time together.

"Yes, they do," I responded. "Otherwise, whatever you are trapping has a greater chance of escape."

"And what if you are trapping many, many things at one time, how important would it be then?"

Puzzled, I replied, "I would think that it would be very important." I could see that Jesus was holding some kind of simple clock with hands, and that it read that it was almost 12:00. It seemed like there were two minutes to go—either 11:58 or two minutes before twelve.

"Which one do you think it is?" He asked, knowing my thoughts.

"Two before twelve," I responded immediately.

"Look it up," He directed.

- The number 2 – conveys the meaning of union, division, or the verification of facts by witnesses.
- The number 12 – symbolizes God's power and authority; perfect, governmental foundation; completeness

Biblestudy.org

"Put the two together and what does it mean?" Jesus asked.

"*The verification of facts by witnesses has been completed before God's power and authority, to form a complete and perfect, governmental foundation*," I said.

"I have told you that I am coming suddenly/quickly. This has been a common theme to many who have been spending time with Me. It will be the speed in which these traps close, in many nations, that will shock and awe the people of the earth. Only I could orchestrate such an operation! No man, no organization and no country could do what I am about to do and get the credit—No, it will be obvious that when I act, it will be a supernatural event!

"Greg, you do not need to know the details. I am letting all of those who have been walking with Me in on this—you will feel a part of it as you see it happen because of what you have invested in partnering with Me. This will add to the explosion of faith that is coming upon the earth."

> Weeping may endure for the night, but joy comes in the morning. Psalm 30:5

~TEN~

Treasures and Resources

The Kingdom of Heaven is like a treasure that a man discovered hidden in a field. In his excitement, he hid it again and sold everything he owned to get enough money to buy the field.

The Kingdom of Heaven is like a merchant on the lookout for choice pearls. When he discovered a pearl of great value, he sold everything he owned and bought it!

Matthew 13:44-46

Yard Treasures July 5/2019

This morning as I looked for Jesus, I could not see Him in the room with me. As I looked out the window of the study, I could see Him moving on the front lawn. He was moving from spot to spot in what appeared to be random order.

"We are un-earthing the treasures that were placed here long ago," Jesus commented casually.

When He said "we" I became aware that there were many of my ancestors (I was not sure who they all were) with shovels and they were digging and finding things in the spiritual realm. Some were sifting and refining what was dug up, but most were digging with shovels. It was very evident that what was being dug up was very valuable and priceless to God's Kingdom.

Uncovering Treasure September 9/2020

As I sat to meet with Jesus, I realized that I hadn't turned the office chair to face me. His voice spoke, "Even though you haven't turned the chair, I am still in the room ready to meet with you."

"What is on Your heart for today?" I asked.

Jesus was standing by the window, looking out at my front yard from the study. "Let's talk about buried treasure. How much treasure do you think that there is to be uncovered?"

I responded, "I think there is a lot, considering You have deposited many things in the earth and that they have been there for a very long time, waiting to be discovered and used."

"That's correct," He said. "And as I teach you to find and utilize these resources, a whole new picture will unfold. You (My Church) are about to discover the unlimited resources that you have at your disposal to empower you and utilize. As you partner with Me, these resources will be released to assist you walking authentically with Me that the world and its systems cannot ignore or push away.

"Do you understand what resources are, Greg? They are sought after and power whole countries. But I tell you that *these* resources, which come from heaven itself, will give My Church power like it has never seen before, even in the early years after My ascension!

"This is because My Church is now a global Church, and it reaches to the far ends of the earth. The time is here to fulfill all that she is called to be, and these resources will empower her mission in these last days."

"How will we know what to look for, LORD?"

"How do you find Me now? You wait upon My Spirit and He moves, one time this way, another time that way. In this same manner He will reveal the resources that are hidden and buried, awaiting discovery for such a time as this. My plans are perfect and My timing is impeccable. This will all happen flawlessly as you seek Me in a spirit of humility and obedience.

"The new alignment that I am bringing to My Church will unlock these treasures and they will be used to spread My glory throughout the earth. Even My angels will be surprised at some of what I show you and give you to use in the days ahead! Be encouraged. Walk in faith. Trust Me to lead you to the green pastures, for I am the good shepherd!"

A Transfer of Wealth September 28/2020

I spent about twenty minutes praying in the Spirit, finally asking Jesus what might be on His heart.

"Faith is rising," He said, sitting still in silence.

"It sure doesn't seem like faith is rising. All around us I see people struggling from all kinds of issues," I lamented.

"Greg, do you think faith rises in the good times? Do people seek Me out when they think they have things under control?"

"No, I suppose they don't," I replied.

"And what about you? Where is your faith at?" He prodded.

"LORD, I am so easily shaken, depending on the circumstances and the people's countenance around me."

"So where is your focus?" Jesus persisted.

"Yes, during those times I get lost in what's around and happening to me and I forget to look to You and what You have promised me," I answered.

Jesus began to teach me. "Your flesh is not going to want to follow Me in this way (by faith). It is always going to prefer comfort, cushion, safety and the ability to manage on your own. But I offer a better way. One that is a true pathway and free of dead ends. It really is a highway to holiness to follow Me by faith, to trust in My provision for you in all things, in all ways. I do own the cattle on a thousand hills and will provide for you enough and at the right time. This is a truth that I am about to prove to not only you, but My greater Church body. You will see that you can't out-give Me!

"If My Bride is to really know Me, they must know My generous nature. Abundance always flows from My throne, and I direct it to anyone I please. Those with the faith to ask not only receive, but are enabled with a capacity to handle what I give to them. This too, will be something that the Church learns in this season.

"My storehouses are bursting with resources for this coming movement and I am about to release great spiritual wealth to those who hunger and thirst for it. Even in the physical, there will be a great transference of wealth from those who have un-righteously gained profit, to those who have stood uprightly.

"Faith is rising, Greg, though you may not see it now. But there is a great wave coming that soon all will see. Hold your ground! Stand firm and focus on Me!"

The Exponential Resource of Prayer December 30/2020

As I petitioned God in the quiet of the walk-in closet in the middle of the night and digesting the truth of God fighting for us, I began to understand the call to be up praying at this time. We know that covens and other groups that practice witchcraft often release their curses—really demonic, destructive prayers—at 3 a.m.

While this is the darkest time of the night, providing the optimum environment for covert petitions against God's people, I believe the LORD is pointing to a better reason to get up and pray. If one person is up praying wholeheartedly for righteousness to break forth, he/she puts a hundred times the amount of wicked enemy forces on the run. But if even one more joins that person uniting in prayer (despite living in different geographic locations) the number of evil plans that are scattered goes up exponentially! No wonder Jesus is wooing us to prayer and drawing closer to Him!

Following My thoughts as I wrote them down, Jesus began to speak into this. "Greg, this is why the battle has turned in your favor! You have been joining with others in battling back the enemy and they are suffering great losses. With each battle that is won, strongholds have been taken down and resources seized and returned to My Kingdom. I told you earlier that we were at a tipping-point—a place where the fight would turn in your favor.

This has happened, just like at Normandy where a beachhead was secured, but now it is time to continue with the campaign. The enemy has held vast territories and powerful, vehement structures that take time to overcome and destroy. There will also be the need for re-building and re-structuring ahead that will only be successful under My guidance. That is where My Hidden Ones will play a prominent role in the restoration that is to come.

"You have always known that coming to Me in prayer is never a waste of time, but now you are beginning to understand just how important this has been, and will continue to be, moving forward. Be diligent in coming to Me! I will not only teach you more, but have you in turn, teach others what I have revealed to you. Stay the course!

Stewarding the Treasures January 2/2021

> But Mary treasured up all these things and pondered them in her heart. Matthew 2:19

> But His mother (Mary) treasured all these things in her heart. Luke 2:51

"Jesus," I asked, "tell me more about treasuring your mysteries."

"Greg, there are treasures that are more valuable than anything, any substance, any currency that you can find on the earth. Mary became aware from the outset of her pregnancy that something of great value was happening in her life. Though she had no reference, nothing to compare to or wise person to seek out, her spirit was in tune to My Spirit. She made the conscious choice to keep these mysteries and the experiences that were happening supernaturally close to her heart; to not allow them to dissipate or be forgotten.

"I can tell you that because she valued these experiences and memories, in time she came to understand the relevance and true interpretation of each one, and they became the treasures of her heart. When recounting these times, she became well aware of the value in the revelation given her and gave them their just deserve.

"My Church will learn to treasure these mysteries as they unfold in the coming days. You, and others like you, have been given treasures like this already as frontrunners, so you must be good stewards of these valued possessions if they are to hold their value in the eyes of My Church. Both Matthew and Luke mention this in their accounts of Me, so you can be assured that this is an important aspect of ministering to My heart in how you manage the mysteries as they unfold. Know that I will help you all to treasure these things as long as you truly partner and stay in step with Me and the angelic support that I send to you.

"When you steward My treasures well and cherish them in this way, all other kinds of wealth and resources follow in the natural. This, too, is a key that will unlock much before you in the coming days."

~ELEVEN~

Heavenly Books

You watched me as I was being formed in utter seclusion, as I was woven together in the dark of the womb.

You saw me before I was born. Every day of my life was recorded in your book.

Every moment was laid out before a single day had passed.

Palm 139:15, 16

The Book of Wonders July 2/2019

I spent some time praying through my prayer for the spiritual environment and looking for Jesus. I picked up my previous journal and read through a large section of it.

I asked Jesus if I should once again go ask for permission to subdivide our acreage, from the farm land that we own.

"Greg, why would you do that?" He asked me.

My sense was that He still very much had plans for the acreage to stay intact as a whole.

Jesus said, "I have a book open for you, Greg."

"What is the purpose of the book, LORD?"

"It is part of what I am doing in these times, and you are in it. I want to encourage you to seek Me and encourage others to seek Me, for I will be found! I call this the *Book of Wonders*."

The Book of Discovery July 28/2019

I asked the LORD what was on His heart for the day and His insight into the delay of our local church receiving our building permits from the city. It seemed that there was something about the lines of spiritual power that He had been showing me for months that were having some negative effect on moving forward. I knew that the location of the church site was a major intersection of a number of these spiritual lines.

"Greg, you are very close to putting this all together."

"LORD, I do not want to be a lone ranger in confronting this," I commented.

Jesus looked down at a now-visible open book on His lap. "Greg, you are in this book."

I queried, "What book is this?"

"*The Book of Discovery*," He stated.

The Book of Discovery Again August 16/2019

Jesus' voice broke in asking, "Why did I show you the *Book of Discovery*?"

"Well LORD, there is something that you want me to see."

"And do you think that I would reveal it to you if it wasn't important for this time?" Jesus continued.

I sat silently with this, knowing it was right.

"What if I revealed something to you that was absolutely key to My Bride moving forward—a necessary thing for the advancement of the Kingdom?"

"It would have to be Christ in me that would need to take that on—otherwise I am bankrupt!" I answered honestly.

"When you are ready, I am going to download this to you—and nothing is going to be the same for you or the Church. You didn't want to write 'that' down because you are afraid of change. But I tell you that once this comes, you will not be able to believe how you managed without it! You think it is going to be difficult to get 'there' but I tell you it will be like entering a pool of warm water.

"I told you that you were in the *Book of Discovery* and this will take place. Greg, understand that you are just part of the intricacies of My plan laid down in the foundations of the earth from the beginning—a plan that is about to ripen and be fulfilled."

The Book of Things to Come September 10/2019

As I was studying the book of 1 John, I began to sense that Jesus was sitting across from me, with a book open on His lap. "You think that this is the *Book of Discovery* that you saw before. This one is different; this is called the *Book of Things to Come*. You are afraid of the shaking that must take place, but look at what shaking does—it settles everything into its right place, creating a firmer foundation. These things must happen if I am to come in My fullness. You must keep your eyes on Me…"

"What else do You want me to know," I asked.

"I love this time we have to spend together. That is one of the reasons that I have you on this sabbatical."

I received a picture in my mind of road repair that was happening in my heart. I sensed that this was the summer season of construction that eventually leads to project completion and better movement and travel.

The Book of Mischief September 29/2019

I sat in the quiet of the morning giving thanks to God for being able to attend a men's event with both of my sons at our church the previous evening. Even before I could ask where Jesus might want to meet with me, I could tell that He was sitting in the chair across from me. On His lap was a book and it was closed, back cover facing up. There was a definite sense that the book had been closed, and/or completed.

I asked the LORD what the book was called and heard Him say that this was the *Book of Mischief.* I thought to myself, "This can't be right, that's not a holy book." But almost immediately I sensed a rebuff from Jesus and the direction to look the meaning of the word *mischief.*

According to Merriam-Webster, mischief means:

- A specific injury or damage to a particular agent
- A cause or source of harm, evil, or imitation
- Action that annoys or irritates
- The quality or state of being mischievous

"From this point on Greg, you are going to see a marked difference in the focus and potency of the prayers of the saints. I am turning off the tap, so to speak, in allowing the enemy to confuse your purpose and intent so that what you are asking Me to act on will be clear to you."

The Book of Adventure May 6/2020

I spent time asking Jesus the three questions that I quite often ask Him when we meet together. As my focus on Him improved, I could see that Jesus had a book open and I knew that it was called the *Book of Adventure*. As I gazed at Him, the LORD communicated a previous statement effortlessly, "…and you are in it." His right hand and forefinger pointed at a place on the open page, and the word "Now" was highlighted.

"You think that you have to wait for the crisis to be over to begin (the adventure) but I tell you that you have already started. That is why you get excited about meeting for prayer and seeing life-change come through deliverance.

"There are new ways and innovations coming, Greg. Do not be afraid of these things as I reveal them, for they will be for the coming of My glory. I will walk with you, hand in hand, every step of the way. Only by walking with Me and My Spirit will you see breakthrough.

"Greg, do not look to the world for solutions. *Now* is the time for the impossible!"

The Books of Action and Hope June 6/2020

This is the day after the June full moon, so I spent some time in cleansing prayer. I sensed that Jesus was in His chair. I also knew that He had a book open on His lap called the *Book of Action*, but right away it became apparent that there was a second book open under the first called the *Book of Hope*. Jesus was pointing to a spot in the top book and I heard Him say, "Now is the time…"

Somehow, I sensed I could carry on what He was saying, knowing that it was time for action.

"LORD, what action are we supposed to take?" I asked.

"Greg, there is a strong correlation between the action that needs to be taken and the hope that lies underneath. One must happen before the other is released. Sometimes you think that this action is something that *you* must do, when really all that I am asking is for you *to pray* that the action is taken. Can you do this?

"Yes, LORD, I can," I responded. I spent time praying both in English and in the Spirit. As I did this I watched as Jesus flipped the pages forward in the *Book of Action.*

Three Books Open August 7/2020

As I sat with Jesus this morning, I knew that He had three books open that lay, one on top of the other, on His lap. The bottom book was the *Book of Adventure*, the middle was the *Book of Advancement*, and the top volume was the *Book of Annuls*. "Annul" means to declare or make legally invalid or void. Because this book was on top and appeared to be open to a newer page, it seemed like this annulment was about to happen soon. It seemed like the order of the books was important. The top would be dealt with first, the middle second and finally, the bottom.

Jesus began to speak to this. "Greg, once I declare what the enemy tried to sow in creating chaos, fear and disruption over the past months annulled, there will be a great advancement of My Kingdom and all that comes with it. This advancement cannot be stopped, but it *can* be mishandled if My leaders don't understand the times. I have raised up many like you who come to spend time with Me every day to understand how I am moving in this New Day. The (angelic) garrison is proof that not only is this advancement under way, but that it is a very real thing—as you all are about to experience!

"I have told you before that your name is in the *Book of Adventure*. This, too, is about to take flight! As you see the annulment of the enemy's plans and witness the advancement of My royal armies, you will be swept up in a wave of adventure. Your destiny—all that you were created for—is about to catch up with you!"

As I looked at Him, Jesus began to close the books, one at a time, and lay them on the floor by His feet. Then He extended His hand toward Me and began to pray. I prayed in the Spirit, agreeing with what He was praying over me.

The Book of Adventure Again August 18/2020

Jesus opened with a question. "Why would I tell you that you are in the *Book of Adventure*, Greg?"

"Perhaps somewhere ahead an adventure awaits me?" I surmised.

"What if I told you that you were already in it?"

"LORD, it seems like I'm stuck here at home, with no congregation to meet with and little to no travel to speak about."

"Perhaps your definition of adventure needs to change," Jesus mused.

I spent some time thinking about this. Jesus just gazed intently into my eyes.

"You admitted yesterday that you (and others) are growing rapidly in hearing, seeing and trusting in what I am doing, despite all the indicators of the world speaking a different, counter narrative. If you could take My hand and fly around the world together seeing sites, would you call that an adventure?" Jesus asked me. "Now that I am showing those in My Church (who are earnestly, with perseverance, seeking to understand what I am doing in this hour) My plans for the harvest, does this not seem like an adventure?"

As I looked at Jesus in His chair, I saw that He was holding a small telescope in His hands, the kind that a ship captain of old would use.

"Greg, I see ahead. If I say that you are not only in the *Book of Adventure*, but you have already started the adventure *now*, trust Me! You would not believe what I have in store for you all in the days ahead and you will be part of it."

Somewhat dumbfounded, I asked, "How do I engage in this?"

Jesus answered, "Apart from Me, you can do nothing. Continue to do what you are doing. Spend time with Me. Pray. Encourage others. Stay clear of the pollution of the media. Wait, watch and wonder. This has been spoken over you before but it is extremely relevant in this season. I live in expectation and hope, as this is the bedrock (foundation) of belief. And with belief comes faith, the environment that manifests all of the aspects of My Kingdom. It will be by faith that you enter the adventure in its fullness. Shalom!"

Micah and the Book of Things to Come September 22/2020

It was a clear, fall morning and I went out to the studio to pray. As I sat, I looked around at the empty chairs and sensed that Jesus was there to meet with me, and that we were not alone.

"Jesus, I sense that You have brought someone with You today."

"Yes, Greg," His voice answered.

"LORD, help me to understand this," I said. As I sat there, I began to see that the being with Him was a high-ranking angel. After asking the name, I began to see in my mind *Micah.*

"Greg, Micah is here as your protective angel. He has been assigned to you from the beginning. He has something that he is to give you now," Jesus stated, turning His head to where the angel was.

I looked at the chair Micah was sitting in and it was a book wrapped in ribbon with a bow. "LORD, what is this book?"

Jesus looked at me intently and responded, "It is the *Book of Things to Come.* I am giving it to you through Micah. He is going to assist you and help you understand what is in it. You are coming into the days that I have made for you, Greg, and as long as your eyes are on Me, you will not stumble in prevailing and carrying out all I have called you to. Micah and his company will assist and go before you as I command them to; they will enable the path you are about to embark on to be successful in every way.

"Greg, you have been seeing through the shroud of deception that covers the whole earth right now, but soon the veil will be removed and the whole earth will see the scheme that was being played out by the dark powers on the earth. It was meant to distract and deceive even the most devoted of My followers.

"But you have seen through this because of your time spent with Me and have been willing to declare the New Day. Soon you will be doing this on a much larger scale. That is why I have shown you your escort and have given you this book. As a watchman and a gatekeeper, I have positioned you to speak forth and steward what I plan to do in the days ahead. This is part of what I have you pray when you pray in the Spirit.

"Persevere, because shortly things are going to break open. You will be needed to speak truth and clarity into the mysteries unfolding ahead. Then you will be amazed at the many things that I was doing in and around you that you did not notice. I now pronounce the calling on you and activate it in all of its fullness. Shalom!"

More on Micah September 27/2020

"Let's talk about Micah and the *Book of Things to Come*," Jesus said to me.

"Micah is part of an expeditionary force that I have sent to expedite what is going on now. He has My commissioning to eradicate the powers and principalities that I am disarming. There is going to be work that you do in concert with Micah and the company with him. Together My wishes will be carried out in your region, and yes, beyond as well.

"You cannot see into the *Book of Things to Come* right now. You have sensed some of its contents by drawing into My spirit, but these pages must be opened in order and in the right timing. You have been given this book because someone must turn each page as I ask them to. You have been given the right giftings and temperament to do this, but again I forewarn you to stay in step with Me. There will be a strong temptation to run ahead and turn pages prematurely. This will only result in confusion and a lack of clarity.

"Part of your call, Greg, will be to actually slow others down from acting on things before I have commanded it. You must do this gently and with great tact. It goes without saying that striking out ahead of the general's orders can be catastrophic. Most will understand this when you put it this way.

"The *Book of Things to Come* is a prophetic book; its sequence of events is especially important to its outcome. Therefore, you must be a good steward in all that I reveal, as I reveal it! But do not be anxious about this responsibility, as the closer you draw in to Me, the less you will feel like you have to do anything but spend time with Me in prayer. This is the key and you are already encouraging others to do the same.

"This is going to become a great movement. Never before in history will so many be so devoted to coming to Me in honest, heartfelt two-way prayer. You will be My friends as well as My children. It is My desire that My glory would rest on all who believe in Me and that they would celebrate this fullness of My presence as well in this pre-ordained time."

Jesus continued, "This *is* a New Day and what I will over the earth *will* transpire. I encourage you to look over the promises that I have spoken over you, as they will bring you great comfort and boldness to obey everything that I ask of you in the days ahead. I reveal things to you not just because I want you to know, but because as these things come to pass, your faith will shoot forward in strength.

"Remember when you saw the baptism scene in a vision, that occurred much later at a men's retreat? Do you recall the *sense of awe* that you felt when you realized I was showing you that very thing in the physical? There is so much of that coming to you (and others) Greg! This will build so much confidence in taking to heart what I say to My Church and strengthening your faith, that there will be nothing you cannot do in My Name!

"This is exactly what happened to My early Church. As they began to recollect My words and the promises I had spoken over them, there came an explosion of faith and trust in Me that could not be extinguished! One faith episode led to another, which fed into another still. And as they learned to pair My revelation with My timing, the

Church became an unstoppable force. This is a taste of the experiences that lie ahead."

More on the Book of Things to Come October 29/2020

"Greg, what do you think the first event in the *Book of Things to Come* is?" I was asked by the LORD.

"The miraculous end to the Corona virus," I immediately answered.

"And how will this come about?" He asked again.

"Your Church stops agreeing with the media and begins to decree the truth."

"That is partly right. Remember, I said that as this virus threat is taken away, the greater threat is continuing on in fear and the disorientation that fears brings. Not only is a compass needed, but true north needs to be discerned and noted as well so that bearings can be taken and a position established.

"Greg, I am going to begin to open up the book and it will not only need to be read, but interpreted," Jesus added.

I looked up and realized that He was sitting across from me, smiling, with the unopened book on His lap. He looked like He could open it at any time.

"Things are going to move quickly after the (U.S.) election. You discern correctly that this book will be read after it is over. You wonder how this is all going to transpire, but like all things with Me, the less that you strive on your own and rest in Me, the easier you will find it to stay in step. The faith, courage and boldness that I have been encouraging you to grow and walk in will be used ahead, for without these the assigned tasks would be impossible for you.

"Understand that *I chose you!* And if I have chosen you (and I have!) then I will also empower you by My Spirit if you choose to draw in to Me. You want to know all the details but it is much better that these be revealed in bits and at the proper times. Understand this also; with each page that is turned comes an added dimension to what I am building upon in this hour. They will be turned at the right time and brought before Me in the proper way. This too, will be directed by My Spirit.

"Greg, this *does not* all hinge on you, but rather, your role is part of a greater movement that no force in the universe can stop! I have invited you into the integral components because I desire to, not because I have to. So, enjoy these days, Greg, for these are the days so many of the generations before you yearned to see, but didn't. I say to you, get ready!"

The Book of Things to Come – Page 1 November 15/2020

I spent over thirty minutes praying in the Spirit, when I suddenly realized that Jesus was sitting across from me, waiting to speak.

"Let's open that book now," He directed. "What's on the first page?"

I knew that He was talking about the *Book of Things to Come* so I grabbed my journal and postured myself to listen. "The end of the Covid-19 virus. That is what you told me before."

"Yes, and how do you turn the page on this?" Jesus inquired.

I answered, "You start to decree and declare that the virus is no more. But Jesus, every time I bring this up, people look at me like I am delusional."

"Greg, the delusion is that I *can't* take this away! I am looking for My remnant to stand up and take action. This requires faith! But I tell you where there is even the smallest spark, there can be fire! Speak the truth and watch how this will turn into a mighty blaze! I am going to turn the page on Covid-19 and I will use anyone with even the smallest amount of belief to do this. The wave of declaration has to start somewhere, so why not with you and those that you pray with?"

"Father," I prayed, "I ask that you would help us with our unbelief. In your marvelous grace and mercy, speak to each one that you are calling to in your own, special way, that they would truly know that not only are you calling them to this, but that you will do exactly what you say."

"Greg, this is just the beginning. Wait, watch and wonder as one thing after another turns, changes and falls. You will see My mighty hand and outstretched arm move in ways you have never seen Me move in, and topple things you never thought would be toppled. All of this starts by turning the first page. All of this starts with a spark of faith!"

More About Page 1 November 17/2020

This morning after praying, I looked at Jesus as He sat across from Me. He had what looked like a scroll and He was holding one dowel in each hand. The scroll was half turned to me, so that we could both see it. As I looked closer at the document, I could see the word "Declaration" at the top section.

"LORD, what is this that you are showing me?" I asked.

"Greg, this is the declaration that the Covid-19 virus no longer has any jurisdiction upon the earth. I said that I would turn the page on this and I meant it! From this day forward you will see it start to dissipate, until it completely disappears.

"No one, except those in My Church who have been listening to Me will understand this. Governments will be disoriented as they have been ramping up for a siege. Multi-national companies that are getting ready to roll out the vaccine, will at first, deny that anything has changed and continue to push forward on all fronts. Even the general population will be afraid to move away from the protocols, even though evidence that the virus still exists just isn't there.

"I had you speak to the prayer group on Sunday as a gift to them. Without that jolting word, they would have taken longer to understand that it is I who am acting against the virus. Some believe it now, while others will believe shortly.

"This has all been planned since the beginning of time. You are only a small part of what I am doing around the world through those that I have hidden, like you. They have been doing their part, just as you have."

The Hardest Page to Turn November 26/2020

When I looked over at Jesus sitting in His chair, I could see Him in that now familiar pose of hands out, fingers up and palms toward me. His eyes were closed and it seemed like He was breathing in everything I had prayed earlier that morning. Even when I looked a few minutes later, He was still sitting like this. After a few more minutes of just being still, I sensed His readiness to converse. He reached down beside the chair and picked up a book off of the floor.

"You get nervous every time I bring this book out," He stated. "You shouldn't. For the things that are to come are momentous and life-changing for so many. There is nothing to fear in this!

"Greg, you have opened the first page of this, and your faith wavers as you see absolutely no signs that what I have told you is true. Does this mean that it is not the true reality? You are about to discover what My early disciples discovered—there is great power in speaking this reality forth into the earthly realm!

"Your apprehension this morning in seeing the book was that you were going to be asked to turn the next page. But we are not yet finished with the first one. In fact, this is the hardest to turn in so many ways. Once you have learned what I am teaching you and you share with others, opening the rest of the book will seem rather simple.

"So, let's get back to the crux of the matter: Why does your faith waver? Why is it strong one moment and weak in the next? Why has what I have said to you carry so much weight one day, and seem ridiculous the next?" Jesus asked.

We sat there together in the silence, as I contemplated these questions.

"Greg," He went on, "faith and trust go hand in hand. To walk in any power, both of these must not only be present, but also at the very forefront of your actions. You think that your ministry is called Forefront because of your place at the front of a movement. That is only part of it! It is the true essence of placing faith and trust in Me for all things, that I had in mind for using the name.

> Now faith is the reality of what we hope for,
> The evidence of things unseen. Hebrews 11:1

"It is the assurance and trust in what I have said *will* happen, that in turn leads you to have the confidence and strength to declare what I am manifesting and bringing from heaven to earth," the LORD continued, "It can only happen this way, so faith and trust are paramount!"

"You have a hard time believing that this first page has turned simply because you declared to a few people what I asked you to. But it held great power and that is why you felt push-back from the enemy in the Spirit! Their beachhead of unbelief has been damaged and will continue to give way as I speak to others about this. You are learning the simplicity of this. Believe what I have told you. Wait, watch and wonder!"

The Book of Things to Come – Page 2 December 5/2020

"Let's talk about turning the second page," I heard Jesus say. I knew that He was talking about the *Book of Things to Come.*

"But LORD, I don't see any signs in the physical that Covid-19 is receding…" I complained.

Jesus sat there, calmly watching me. "Greg, do you want to know about the second page?"

"Yes, LORD," I answered, "But I don't have a clue of what this is about."

"What did I say would expedite the dismissal of the virus?" He asked.

"Faith rising in the Church. You said that we held the key"

"That is correct. Ask Me for this to be unleashed over the Body. *Ask* Me…" (Jesus was stressing this last part, and His words, 'You have not because you ask not,' reminded me of the importance of not just sitting around but petitioning Him to bring the change.) "Yes, last night when you were walking the dog you heard Paul's words come to you.

> You wrestle not against flesh and blood enemies, but against rulers and authorities of the unseen world, against mighty powers in this dark world, and against evil spirits in the heavenly places. Ephesians 6:12

"This is why My Church *must ask Me* to eradicate this evil and to round up and take it away. Greg, the second page involves a faith to stand against the base of lies of the enemy that keep many from believing that I can eradicate the injustice brought on by the *now illegal* act of perpetuating the virus.

"This wave of faith will grow out of seemingly nothing—no prayer event, no gathering. Instead, this will rise organically in all of those who are earnestly seeking Me with their time. There is a great realization coming—that is present now—that I am the only way. So, Greg, let us turn the second page… ask Me!"

"Lord God Almighty," I prayed, "I ask you to unleash a great wave of faith over your Church. Stir the hearts of all who are earnestly seeking you to ask you to act against the pandemic and all of the damage that it has brought to the earth. We ask you to reverse the spread and completely and totally eradicate the Covid-19 virus by Your great power in concert with the rising faith of Your people."

The Book of Things to Come – P. 3 & 4 December 11/2020

I sat, focusing on Jesus, and thinking about how much I have changed through the months. I thought about a book I had given away that described the kind of prayer time I was now practicing, when Jesus' voice broke in.

"What if I made that book a best seller?"

"Then I hope it would get into the hands of many people. I don't really care what kind of revenue it would produce," I answered.

"And this is how you have changed. You have become Kingdom minded, which always puts others first," He replied. I could see that He had the *Book of Things to Come* open on His knees and it looked like He was set to turn another page. "What page did we turn to open the book and why did it seem so difficult to do?" Jesus queried.

"It was the end of the Covid-19 virus, and it seemed so difficult to turn because there was such a stronghold of unbelief that it could happen without the widespread use of a vaccine. That was the great narrative that was spun over us from the beginning," I replied.

"Yes," Jesus said, "and what was the next page that I had you turn?"

"You had me ask that faith would be unleashed in the Body of Christ that would act as a base to stand against and erode this enormous lie. It is a groundswell move of faith that You are the only way."

"Correct again," He said. "This is happening behind closed doors all across your region and beyond. Now, do you want to turn the third page?"

"Of course, I do," I answered, "But I don't have a clue as to what this is."

"Actually, you do," He responded. "What was the verse of the day on your bible app?"

> Haughtiness goes before destruction;
> Humility precedes honor. Proverbs 18:12

"We are really turning two pages at once here, Greg. Ask Me to bring action and judgement upon all of those who have been acting haughty and arrogant, especially who have despised Me, My laws and My people. Secondly, ask Me to honor all of those who have honorably served and walked in My ways, upholding righteousness for the sake of My Kingdom. Ask Me to strengthen them as they stand like stakes in the ground upholding justice and right standing with Me. Ask Me to infuse them *all* with boldness, courage and power which is of supernatural origin, emblazed with My holy fire, so that all the proud and arrogant who would dare to oppose them would be immediately burned up before them."

Micah is Sent December 19/2020

Last night I just happened to open my eyes and look at my clock. It read 3:00. I shot out of bed, realizing that this was a direct invitation from the LORD to get up and pray.

As I prayed in the Spirit, it didn't take long until I had a feeling like what I was saying was important—like a lawyer arguing in a courtroom. After singing a song, the tone changed to where I sensed I was in the dying moments of a court case—into the final address. In the midst of praying, I started addressing the LORD as *Adonai*, and I knew that this was extremely significant to what I was saying. Later the next morning I looked up that particular name of God, finding it to mean "Master".

Somehow, I knew my late-night prayer time was coming to a close and I was thanking the LORD and praising Him. As I did this and prepared to return to bed, His voice broke in saying, "Micah is sent." I made a note in my mind to remember this phrase and look up what Jesus had told me about this angel in earlier visits. I knew He had been sent to assist and direct me in the days ahead, but couldn't remember much more.

As I read through my journal the next morning, I came across this passage from a second visit about this angel that I received in September.

Jesus had said: "Micah is part of an expeditionary force that I have sent to expedite what is going on now. He has My commissioning to eradicate the powers and principalities that I am disarming. There is going to be work that you do in concert with Micah and the company with him. Together My wishes will be carried out in your region, and yes, beyond as well."

Yesterday, the LORD said He would bring a sign and that I wasn't to look for it, but that He would bring it to

Me. He told Me it would bolster my faith in an incredible way. "Jesus, it has!"

The Book of Things to Come – Page 5 December 22/2020

Last night I joined Jesus for prayer at 3:25 a.m. At one point, I slowed down what I was speaking and heard Him say, "Now is the time for precision." At that time, I took my time with the words that were coming to me by the Holy Spirit.

Near the end of our time together, I found myself repeatedly speaking out, "If God is for us, who can ever be against us?" This gave me great peace as I returned to bed.

Yesterday was also the Winter Solstice, the turn-around day where the days start to become longer, the amount of light increases daily, while darkness decreases. The Christmas Star also appeared last night, though the cloud cover in our region prohibited us from viewing this incredible phenomenon.

"What do you think is next?" Jesus asked from His chair.

"I think that we are to turn another page in the *Book of Things to Come,"* I answered.

"That is correct. And do you know what that is?"

I began to think through the pages that we have turned together already:

1. The end of the virus
2. A wave of faith released
3. Action and judgement against the haughty and arrogant
4. Honor to those who serve and walk in your ways

"LORD," I said, "I'm sensing that Page 5 has to do with the sign of the star and that it is important, as there is so much spiritual opposition coming at me right now as I try to understand you correctly."

"Greg, it is as simple as this: Pray that all the wise men (and women) that I am raising up in this hour would come to worship Me. That *all* of these key individuals would see what I am about to do and understand that it is only I who can bring about such a thing. I must get the credit for this turn-around and it starts with the testimony of some key individuals.

"There is so much opposition coming against My people at this moment, but all of this is about to change in the blink of an eye! Pray for those wise people that I have strategically placed all around the world, in every nation and speaking every tongue. From these beachheads My holy network will spread out and the rescue operation will be underway. I am moving against this evil scheme that has been set into motion by wicked people. There will be no takeover of My people and I am coming against the virus. This plan will be turned on its head! The great serpent will roar no more, as he has had his day and failed. He will retreat to lick his wounds and to wait for another opportunity to ascend to power.

> But those who trust in the LORD will find new strength. They will soar high on wings like eagles. They will run and not grow weary. They will walk and not faint.
>
> Isaiah 40:31

At this, the LORD took me into a time of prayer with Him, praying in the Spirit, praying the above passage over those wise men and women, decreeing that the fifth page was turned.

The Book of Things to Come – Page 6 December 31/2020

"Let's turn another page," I heard the LORD say. He had the book open and sitting on His lap as it had been in previous encounters. I knew this was His agenda for the morning, but could feel my hesitancy in engaging in this. I sensed that Micah—the commanding angel assigned to me and the task of turning the pages—was standing on the deck behind Jesus' chair, looking in at us through the glass of the window. Behind was a whole company of angelic troops waiting patiently on our front lawn.

"What is the next page that must be turned, Greg?" Jesus asked me.

"LORD, as always I need your guidance," I said.

"What was the verse of the day that was sent to you this morning?" He quizzed me.

> We can make our plans, but the LORD determines our steps. Proverbs 16:9

"Greg," Jesus continued, "we are turning the page on the agenda and plans of the enemy. This great uprising, with all of its covert operations and partners is about to crumble. This will happen before your eyes. The scope and magnitude of this scheme was simply too large and too grand for the enemy to manage. Pride and haughtiness have caused this grand delusion to begin to fall in on itself. This is beginning to happen now but you will really begin to see the collapse in January.

"So, let's turn the page. Pray that I would now determine the steps for all leaders, in all realms of the world. They have made their plans, but I—God Almighty—determines next steps and it will be so! I give you the ability to commission Micah and his troops to action this next phase in all of its fullness.

"Greg, pray for all of those who know better than to follow the delusion, but are in danger of being trapped in the rubble and debris of the collapse. Angels of mercy travel ahead of My justice, seeking all who would have a heart to honestly turn and seek truthfully the path of righteousness. We are turning the page on this evil plan.

> A king detests wrongdoing, for his rule is built on justice. Proverbs 16:12

"My justice must come, as a righteous kingdom demands it. It is no secret that we are turning this page at the end of a difficult year. There must be a turn-around from everything that has ruled the day. This page *must* be turned!" Jesus proclaimed.

The Book of Things to Come – Page 7 January 6/2021

I spent an extended time of praying in the Spirit, when the LORD's voice broke in.

"Greg, I have the book open, and you may be surprised at the next page that you are about to turn."

"Jesus, I have no idea what it is. As always, I need your help in this," I responded.

"Well, what was the last page that we turned together?" He prodded.

Thinking back, I said, "It was the last day of the year and You asked me to turn the page on the agenda and plans of the enemy. And LORD, I believe by faith that this was done."

"And what did I reveal to you the very next day?" Jesus asked.

"You showed me a celebration and you wore a party hat and blew a party favor toward me," came my answer.

"So, what is the next page about?"

"A victory celebration! You want me to turn the page of victory!" I cried out with excitement.

"This is just the beginning of the pages we will turn together, Greg. But be encouraged. I always win! So, when the Church partners with Me like she is learning to, and petitions Me with honest, heartfelt prayer and positions herself in repentance and humility, seeking purity, there is nothing that can stand against her. I am reforming My true worshippers. They are the ones who have refused to let go of the hem of My garment, but have clung to Me as the darkness came in on all sides. Now I am removing the darkness and light will own the day! All that had been hidden will be out in the open for all to see.

"Yes, Greg, decree and proclaim the victory celebration, for evil has risen up only to be driven back by righteousness! Micah and his forces have joined many others to accomplish this, but soon he will be returning to you for the next assignment. There is much yet to do, so continue to make yourself available and stay in step. Wonderful days are ahead!"

The Book of Things to Come – Page 8 January 14/2021

High winds had made the previous day's snow drift and our rural road was impassable. I spent a good deal of time clearing it so that my wife could drive to work. Finally, I sat down and spent time in prayer and reading scripture. I looked over and knew that Jesus was waiting for Me to look for Him, and once again I noticed the open book on His lap.

"It's time," He said.

I knew that this was about turning another page. I wondered where Micah and his angelic forces were, and of course, Jesus knew my thoughts.

"Micah is at the back (of our house, at the garrison) replenishing. Your property allows them to quickly and efficiently restore all that they will need to return to battle. He (Micah) is listening to our conversation as he oversees this," Jesus said casually. He sat there, His hand on the page and anticipating its turn by holding the upper corner.

I sat for a minute, looking at Jesus and the open book, when suddenly the revelation of what was on the next page came to me.

"LORD, you are calling us to proclaim your coming!" I said excitedly. "It is finally time to proclaim the *coming and arrival* of the New Day!"

In one easy movement His hand moved forward and the page flipped over. As always, Jesus never stopped looking at me with tremendous love in His eyes as He did this. His hand rested fully open on the freshly turned parchment, and there was such peace in the room as we shared that moment together.

I prayed, "By the power and authority that You have given me, Lord Jesus, I declare and proclaim that You, O Mighty God, are ushering in the New Day and every good thing that comes with it, both in the spiritual and the natural. Your Kingdom come on earth, as it is in heaven."

Suddenly Micah appeared standing in the room between us, his hand resting on the LORD's shoulders. He was splendidly attired and I knew that He was pleased with what had just transpired and stood, waiting for his Commander's order to move out with his angelic troops. He was completely refreshed and battle ready. As I sat looking at this, Jesus once again knew my thoughts. He caught me wondering how long this would take before we witnessed this in the natural realm.

"Shortly," was all that I was offered.

The Book of Things to Come – Page 9 January 22/2021

I had trouble connecting with the LORD, so I spent time in Spirit-led prayer regarding some pressing matters. I sensed I was to bind and send away certain spirits (by name) that were involved in this blockage. For some reason, I called upon Micah and his company to assist in this.

"Let's talk about the next page," Jesus said as things cleared, and I knew He wanted to talk about the *Book of Things to Come*. "This will be the last page turned in this chapter. Do you know what this page is?"

I sat for a while, pondering this question. "I know that the last page to be turned ushered in the New Day." Then, like a flash, I understood what this last page was about. "Jesus, your Church must see this New Day for what it really is!"

"Yes, Greg," He replied. "It is one thing to bring the New Day forth, but it is another thing all together for My Church *to see it for what it is by faith*, and fully embrace all that this change encompasses. For many, the change that is about to happen—despite it being so good—will be too much for them to handle and take in. The drastic turn-around that will occur around them will add to the disorientation that the storm of deception brought. Trust in anything will be hard to come by, and it must be My Church that leads the way in believing that this change is from Me and that *I really am good*! As simple as it seems, trusting that anything could ever be good again will be hard to grasp by many, as the wave of exposure and the depths of the evil that was over you come to light.

"So, this is an extremely important page to turn, and I am going to help you with its turning! Pray along side of Me that My Church will truly see Me in this. This New Day is one of the greatest gifts that I will ever give to mankind, and it has been given to your generation! Pray that it will be fully embraced and understood in the context of My good character and love!

"This ends the chapter and puts a close on the season of the storm, says the Lord God Almighty!"

~TWELVE~

LORD, What About Canada?

He shall have dominion also from sea to sea,
    and from the River to the ends of the earth.
Those who dwell in the wilderness will bow before Him,
    and His enemies will lick the dust.
Psalm 72:8, 9 NKJV

Dismantling Powers June 26/2019

This morning I asked Jesus what was on His heart. After a while I sensed that He was standing to my left. He had his scepter in His right hand and held His left hand out, fingers up and palm forward. The hand seemed to be sucking things into it (like a spiritual vacuum) rather than imparting something.

When I asked Jesus about this (He was facing Southeast) He said, "I am dismantling powers and principalities. You moved something like this off the land (beside the church) yesterday and you will do even greater things."

Writing a New Chapter July 1/2020

As I looked for Jesus this morning, I sensed Him sitting in His chair holding an old, non-electric typewriter on His knee.

"I am writing a new chapter for you," He said. "This will be a chapter in your life where all the secret schemes of the enemy that I have shown you over the years will be openly exposed *and accepted*. I will make you a credible and respected resource if you follow Me into this. I am writing (adding) you into the script for these times and you will play an important role if you follow Me.

"There are very few others that have demonstrated a willingness to not only come to Me regularly but truly listen to what I have to say and act on it. You have been faithful in this despite little or no recognition (in a worldly sense) for your efforts. That is ok, because I have seen! That is why I can trust you with what is about to come next. Guard yourself from earthly recognition and all the traps that come with it. Rather, come to Me and I will lead you the entire way.

Jesus continued, "You are a prized possession and precious to Me, Greg! Guard your heart against unbelief and allow the work of the Holy Spirit to grow your faith!"

My Hands are Tied July 13/2020

I spent some time praying, then reading a book on revival. Finally, I put it down to look for Jesus. I sensed Him sitting in His chair, and He encouraged me saying, "You have never seen this before." As I looked at Jesus, it was as if His hands were tied with a thick rope as they rested on His lap.

I thought, "This can't be right. Jesus is all powerful!" So, I checked the Spirit showing me this and it was Jesus! As I stayed with this, the saying, "My hands are tied," came to my spirit and I understood that Jesus was trying to tell me that decisions had been made (it seemed by people) that appeared to keep Him from acting. Just as I was considering this, He simply took His hands and moved them apart, instantly and easily snapping the thick rope. The phrase, "We will have to wait until the (Covid-19) vaccine is released for things to go back to normal," came immediately to my mind. This had been spoken by a friend yesterday and I knew this was being repeated by many, many people around the world—the rope that was tying Jesus' hands.

Very sternly, the LORD looked at me and said, "I told you that as quickly as it came, it would go away. DO NOT agree with this statement!"

The Canadian Church September 29/2020

Last night I finished reading *The Harbingers II*. Jonathan Cahn makes a compelling case that the appearance of Covid-19 is very much linked to the legislation of abortion in America.

"Jesus," I asked when we met, "is there anything that You want to speak into with regard to this or similar?"

"Greg, Canada has its own timeline of if/then… My prophets in Canada are in place and have been acting from the 'background', but soon they, too, will come to prominence at the right time.

"While Canada and the U.S.A. have always been closely linked, they are on two different timelines. But like you have just read, your country has 'hot spots' that are not far off from judgement unless there is a turn-around. This is why My Church must re-align with Me in order to handle the harvest as I intend. 'The harvest is great, but the workers are few,' so much is depending on how well My Church adapts to My ways in the coming days, Greg. How much of the harvest will be taken into the barns before I must act in judgement?

"The Seattle-Vancouver disaster that you saw years ago is not far off unless there is a true turning to Me. There are other things that will be averted in your country, depending on how much My Church embraces the new direction that I am sending her in. This is an unpopular word and many will rebuff this. Hold your ground! Who do you fear, man or Me? The fear of the Lord is *not* an optional thing to embrace in this season. Those that do not revere Me more than what others think will be tossed about like a ship in a storm. Many will lose their way because they have lost this and succumbed to what is actually false.

"The Canadian Church is coming to a moment of its own; it will either choose to be a lamp on a stand, or bow to the steady stream of false truths that the world is sending its way. It must stand on the Word and what My Spirit is saying. This will be counter to everything that the world system is conveying, but be steadfast! For the wave of My glory *is coming* and it will carry all those who are clearly watching for Me to come in this manner!

> Here on the earth, you will have many trials and sorrows. But take heart, because I have overcome the world. John 16:33

A Different Plan for Canada October 12/2020

After spending time with the LORD where He gave me a number of personal directives to follow, He spoke for a brief time about Canada.

"I have a completely different plan and strategy for your nation than I do for your neighbor (USA). Yet there are many similarities and My Church must be ready for what transpires after the Winds of Change cease. You *do* have a job and it is to respond to My call, day or night, to pray into what I have directed you to. Stand in the gap, lift your hands and pray! You *are* going to see victory, but only if you respond to My call."

More on Canada and the USA October 31/2020

"Greg, Satan really believes he has the upper hand right now. But just as I drew the warriors of Ai out of their city, so too am I drawing the agents of the enemy out of the darkness and into the light. We are at a trigger-point—a place of tipping. But I am seeing the remnant in My Church respond and this is making a difference, both in the U.S. and your country.

"There are important events still to occur in America that must take place before you begin to see the great stirring in Canada and other countries around the world. The Americans are leaders in many areas, so what transpires there will spill over into other countries and regions around the world. Continue to pray for them!"

Sweeping Changes Coming November 14/2020

"Well, LORD, I don't set the agenda, You do. What do You want to discuss this morning?"

"I have many things that I want to talk to you about, but one is important for today. What time did I finish the timeline that I gave you with?"

"You said 8:12. This was a different take in '12 after 8' that you spoke before this," I responded.

"And what does 8:12 mean?" He prompted.

"The creation of God's perfect government foundation is completed."

"So how do you understand this today?" Jesus asked.

"I believe that you have completed installing the exact spiritual understructure for your coming Kingdom to rest on. Not only will the governments of the world find position on this, but all facets of culture will be based on this as well—including your Church."

"So, should you have any angst regarding what is going on south of the border?" He asked me knowingly.

"No, LORD."

"And what about your country? Does this not give you some idea as to what I am about to do here as well? I tell you that there are sweeping changes coming to Canada too. By this time next year, the changes you see at all levels of government will be astounding. All will be done to quickly and obediently fall in line with My mandate for this time. I—the LORD—have spoken!"

The Great Reform December 2/2020

I struggled in the silence to connect with Jesus, and finally just sat there in the quiet.

"We can just sit here together for a while, can't we," I heard Him say softly.

"LORD, I feel such an irritation with all of the Covid-19 narration and rhetoric coming at Western Canada as the numbers appear to be rising," I replied, frustrated.

Jesus sat across from me calmly. "Do I look like I am distressed over this in any way? Greg, I have told you things would get worse before they get better—and they are. I have said that the enemy is going to throw more things at you as he loses his grip—and he has. And I have told you that the media will try to extend the effects of the virus even after it has been taken away—and they will. I have told you that the virus is now waning. I have also said that it only takes a few with the faith to believe that I am moving for this to transpire, and I tell you that I have more than enough of My faithful ones! Rejoice in this!

"The great reveal and reversal is taking place right now. You were worrying about your country, its leadership and the general perception that your people are just following along with what is being done. But I also tell you this, along with the sweeping changes that will take place next year, you will also see great reform. The enemy has tried to pollute and distort My dominion—even to give the term a bad name. But Canada was built on the foundation of existing as a country of God-fearing people from sea to sea to sea. Part of the assignment of My New Day prophets is to direct My people back to this vision.

"Do not focus on what is being 'pushed' at all levels right now—because it is about to fall like a house of cards. Instead, trust in what I have said and what I am saying now. Empathize with your leaders, especially those trying to lead My Church. You will need to walk in their favor in the days ahead. Continue to encourage others with humility and grace."

> But the time is coming—indeed it's here now—
> when true worshippers will worship the Father in
> spirit and in truth.
> The Father is looking for those who will worship
> Him in that way. John 4:23

Exposure, Exposure! December 8/2020

As soon as I sat down and looked for Jesus, He began to speak. "Exposure! Exposure! Exposure, Greg. I am bringing exposure! You think that not much is happening around you, other than bits and pieces of what you see about the election. But I tell you it is like I have pulled the plug on the drain of the pool and every crooked and dirty thing *will* be exposed!

"Greg, this is a worldwide thing, not just an American event. There are those around you (your province and region) that are getting very nervous at all that is transpiring. The longer the false narrative of the virus, the corresponding restraints and its effects goes on, the more exposed those who have agreed with the evil one will be. They will have to stick their necks out further and further in order to keep the ruse going.

"Remember the rise of the whistleblowers we spoke about earlier? They are about to pop to the surface, first as a few and then in greater numbers as their courage grows. Like bubbles rising to the top, they will be unable to contain all that they have seen and heard. It will be their sheer numbers that will be irrefutable and that the powerful few in each region will be unable to contain, as a righteous anger arises in the masses that is understandable and natural in response to the great injustice that has been propagated.

Jesus intensely continued on, "Be patient! There is an allotted time for this to take place and a fulfillment that must be reached in order for everything that I predestined to fall into place. It is hard for you to write that (predestined) but there is nothing that I have not seen coming ahead of time. That should be assurance enough to have confidence in what I have spoken to you—both today and in the past. I am the same yesterday, today and forever, so trust that I not only 'have this' but everything that is worrying so many people all over the world.

"Yes, I am separating the wheat from the tares. I am allowing the weeds to grow big and tall; they will stand out from the wheat and that will be their downfall. The harvest is coming and all will be put to the sickle. My holy fire is coming to burn up anything that cannot stand before My glory. Shudder at My omnipotence, O earth! Gape in the holy awe of My splendor as it moves over the land. Get ready, for I am coming!"

Concern Over Canada December 10/2020

"Greg, why do you think you are walking in such peace right now?"

"I believe that you have told me that I was already standing on the far shore, waiting for others to join me from out of the storm," I responded.

"That's right," Jesus agreed. "How good it will be for those who trust in Me *right now*, that believe with all of their heart, soul mind and strength that I am moving *now* against the darkness! How much more will their faith be strengthened as all that I have spoken through the prophetic voices comes to pass!

"Again, you are concerned with what is transpiring with your country. I say to you, don't be! Just as everything that could be shaken is being shaken, everything that must be exposed *is being* exposed. There is no place on the earth that this is not taking place because this involves the enemy's network and plans. This includes Canada and the great revelation that will occur at all levels and in many facets of your society. If I am cleaning house in America, you can rest assured that I am doing the same thing with her neighbors! You already know the scope and magnitude that is involved in bringing My glory forth, the preciseness of My plan and the intricacies of what I have laid down on the true foundation of the earth. All the hubris must be revealed and pulled up so that the weight of My sovereign glory may rest firmly in place. The New Day that is here requires this, and it will be so!

"Watch as you begin to see others around you reach the opposite shore of belief and proclaim the new reality, even in the midst of what appears to be the darkest days yet. Then watch to see what I do with a small remnant of those who know in their heart that I am at work and doing something far beyond anyone's understanding!

"Continue to pray in the Spirit when you can. Call on Me. Seek My face in all that you do. Your Rescuer comes and He will not relent! Watch in wonder as heaven invades earth! Stay strong!"

Bubble Up in Alberta December 12/2020

"Is this where you want to meet today, LORD?" I asked, looking at the chair that He normally sits in when we meet.

"Yes, this is where we usually meet. Greg, your heart is heavy this morning and it shouldn't be. Despite the oppressive blanket that lays over your region right now, it is coming to an end. I tell you, watch for signs that *I have come* (yes, underline that) suddenly/quickly to move against the oppression caused by the virus and everything associated with it. Do not be afraid to write this, but record it with great joy for it will be part of My holy gift to you in the coming days.

"Now let Me remind you that those that are cooperating with the dark agenda will do their utmost to keep things looking like they are still going from bad to worse. Through the media they will continually feed false numbers even as the infection rates dry up and hospitalizations change from active Covid-19 cases to flu and other normal respiratory issues for the time of year. This must happen to separate the sheep from the wolves, and with the agenda's end game in sight, those promoting the collusion with the web of other worldly powers will unknowingly expose their evil scheme further. They are too far to turn back but have yet to reach their desired target.

"At just the right time My light will come upon all that they have desired to keep in the darkness. And when this happens, the disorientation that I have often spoken about will be in your midst. That is when there will be a need for My voices to step forward and bring clarity and direction to what has happened and more importantly, what I am doing!

"Then you will see the dawn of the New Day arise unlike anything you could dream or imagine. As the realization of how I have acted and what I am doing grows, the joy and celebration will be uncontainable. Pray for your premier, as he will be one of the few who remain standing when this is all over.

"Greg, this is why Alberta will be one of the first to break out of this! I must have leadership that honors Me and My ways, and despite the years of things done in darkness and secrecy, there is a remnant in government that I can now work with. Again, this was planned from the beginning and has been evident in the abundant natural resources that I have placed there. Alberta will once again lead the nation back to prosperity as all of the global schemes that have come against her are reversed. This will only happen because My hand is upon your province and I will it to be so!

"Your people and My Church will also lead the nation back to Me. There will be a great outpouring of My Spirit here that will cascade from province to province, but it will bubble up in Alberta like oil gushing to the surface. This is why I have many others, like you, in your region to speak the same message."

Scatter Your Enemies December 21/2020

I was up at 2:55 a.m. this morning again, praying in the Spirit. I had glanced at my phone while watching a movie and noticed a headline that a more serious strain of Covid-19 was on the move. This lined up with a "leaked" agenda and schedule that the Canadian Liberal lead team had allegedly met about in the summer. This made me even more determined to be available to my Lord to pray anytime that He calls.

During my prayer time, I knew that I was warring. At one point I was repeating a phrase that eventually came out in English. It was, "Scatter your enemies and make Your foes flee." (Psalm 68:1) This was a verse that I had memorized when I was a new Christian and leaning spiritual warfare tactics.

The next morning, I continued my habit of reading the entire chapter containing the verse of the day that appears in my bible app. It started with last night's passage!

> Rise up, O God, and scatter your enemies. Let those who hate God run for their lives. Blow them away like smoke. Melt them like wax in a fire. Let the wicked perish in the presence of God.

But let the godly rejoice. Let them be glad in God's presence. Let them be filled with joy. Psalm 68:1-3

Justice is Being Served December 27/2020

As soon as I sat down in my prayer room, the LORD began to speak saying, "Greg, Pharaoh thinks he is winning on all fronts. He delights that his plan continues to move forward, that all of his human counterparts (those that have agreed to be used in the conspiracy) are invested further into this scheme and that many had their Christmas celebration taken from them. Pharaoh is giddy over all of this and hungers for more. This will be his downfall!

"You have heard Me say that I am allowing the necks of those who partner with wickedness to be stiffened, to stand above the rest in haughty arrogance. At the same time, I am calling all who are willing to follow the righteous path to humble themselves and bow at My feet. For My followers, this is about introspection and examining their walk with Me. For those who don't fully know Me yet, but are moving toward My throne, they will begin to experience the mercy and grace of drawing into Almighty God.

"But the haughty and arrogant have already run out of time! I will not stand still and allow the oppression to continue over Canada and all of the other nations any longer! I—Adonai—have spoken! I am a righteous King and My Kingdom is a righteous kingdom! I am coming with My war sword raised and will remove all who stand proudly and arrogantly in their deceitful ways, oppressing My people. For I am coming now as the Judge and not as the Comforter, for there has been a great crime committed that shakes all of the heavens! Justice is being served, and justice must be carried out!"

> Speak up for those who cannot speak for themselves; ensure justice for those being crushed. Yes, speak up for the poor and helpless, and see that they get justice.
> Proverbs 31:8, 9

Jesus continued, "This is coming like rolling thunder and continuous, flashing lightening! There is no escaping My wrath for those who have willingly partnered in this evil plot, so as to gain nothing but power, prestige and position. Yes, I am moving against the powerful and the stiff-necked. Those who are meek and humble and seek to love others will be shown My great mercy and grace. They will not cower in fear as this comes over in swift fashion, but instead will trade in their fear from what has transpired against them, for a holy awe and how I have come to rescue them all. Then you will see the Great Awakening that so many have sought after and others have prophesied about. All of this is about transitioning from darkness to light, evil to goodness, selfishness to true love.

"Greg, the transformation has come! Continue to pray into this, encourage others and stay strong! The first rays of light are here!"

Be Thou My Vision January 5/2021

I woke up this morning humming an old hymn. Later in my quiet time, I was able to look it up: *Be Thou My Vision* (Dallan Forgal 8th century).

> Be Thou my Vision, O Lord of my heart;
> Naught be all else to me, save that thou art
> Thou my best Thought, by day or by night,
> Waking or sleeping, Thy presence my light

"LORD, I am interested in why this hymn is on my heart this morning," I inquired.

"Greg, this is what happens when you live out the lyrics of the first verse—I become your life!" He answered. "My thoughts become your thoughts, what I see, you begin to see. Whether you are awake or sleeping, you are alert to My movement, My ways and My intentions as it relates to you. I am in you and you in Me.

"You have been awakened to more regarding the coming renewal in your country. There is little posted on the internet regarding this because it will be a 'ground up' movement. You have heard Me use the word 'organic' and it will be much like that. Of all the countries of the world, Canada needed to let the ground lay fallow. I am growing an awareness of 'Thy presence, My light' in My people that must be grown from the ground. Therefore, there must be a re-planting of this truth that has died and withered over the years.

"I am speaking to you in song because worship will play a very large role in this awakening. My Spirit will not only live in the worship of My people, but will activate great waves of repentance, consecration and celebration. There will be certain songs that trigger this response—some of older origin and others birthed in the moment of true adoration and devotion. This power of My Spirit moving through music will be one of the trademarks of the Canadian awakening, and will be felt worldwide.

"Everything that you have longed to see—everything you have pursued in seeking renewal for your region—you *will* see and more! So many of the problems that were in Canada before the pandemic—addictions, abuse, family issues, corruption and illicit gain—will mostly disappear in large part to the Church rising in power and influence. And because it is growing naturally from the ground up, it will influence every mountain of Canadian culture and society.

"Again, this will be very disorienting at first, because it will be contrary to how things were for so long. Like finding money on the sidewalk, you want to pick it up but are not sure what the catch is. As things turn on a dime, and all of the current societal issues reverse, there will be few who will know what to do. This is when My Church must be ready to step out and lead the way, interpreting what has transpired and speaking truth. For lies and deception have made so many numb to believing that anything miraculous and beneficial could appear in so quick a time frame.

"Yes, Greg, My Church can expedite the process but only by completely surrendering to the course of allowing Me to be 'their all'. I must be their Vision, the One that they are to look for. For it is only I that am not only the hope of the Church, but the hope of the world as well. Shalom!"

A Great Faith Testimony January 11/2021

Last night I awoke in the middle of the night, but resisted looking at the time. For some reason, I had the last name of the Chief Medical Officer of Canada in my head, and God was speaking to me as I lay there. Finally, I knew that He was calling me to prayer, confirmed when I looked at the clock and it read 3:05.

Once in the prayer closet, I immediately entered into a heightened and fully engaged state of praying in the Spirit. The term 'round up' came to me as I prayed fervently, with both arms moving above my head as if waving swords or swirling lassos. Not only did I get the sense that the CMO was being rounded up for wrong doing (in the spirit), but a nation-wide network of co-

conspirators as well. I asked Jesus about the current national leader, but sensed I was to leave that alone for a time.

Later in my prayer time I was again reminded of the term "fallow ground" and then the Jesus Movement of the early 1970's came to mind. The term "jubilee" was connected to this and highlighted. I realized that there was a connection there that God wanted to point out. I have also noticed a real change in the prayer atmosphere since New Year's!

Jesus began to fill in the blanks of what I had been experiencing in my prayer time the night before. "Greg, there is nothing left of that network (CMO) in the spirit realm now. Despite the earthly position and authority that is in place, all support from the enemy's encampments and structures have been *obliterated* (yes, I wanted you to say that word). My righteous anger has risen to a crescendo and it now will be seen in greater and greater measure!

"As I have spoken to you about many times before, the virus is being taken away as I speak. Last night's strike was devastating to the plans of darkness. This is part of the Great Reversal and a very integral and important piece. You prayed in agreement with many others of My Hidden Ones, who will at some point read this and remember their involvement. These are examples of the things that will bring forth a greater faith, trust and love for Me that will fuel the facilitation of My presence.

"You do not need to understand what exactly went on last night or how it relates to what you see happening in your country today, but only believe that I have seen it all and will react with justice and righteousness.

"Greg, the Canadian Church is asleep on this, but they will soon awaken to the wrong doing and foul play. But

My Hidden Ones have not been fooled—they have seen things for what they were since the darkness rolled in. This is why I have so many prophets and 'watch' men and women. They are the ones who have stood in intercession and refused to let the darkness overwhelm them. And for this there is a great promotion coming that will not be disrupted or thwarted. For boldly proclaiming the truth when no one wanted to hear it, they will be honored!

"I have you write all of this down ahead of My action against the enemy so that there will be a great faith testimony to the Hidden Ones. It will be like the tribute given to the pilots in the Battle of Britain who fought alone in the skies above England while the nation waited. Many, like you, will begin to share all that I was doing during the storm, when many thought I had left them. But you, My Hidden Ones, made all of the difference!"

The Spiritual Waves January 18/2021

I spent considerable time praying in the Spirit. As I felt my time in this winding down, I heard the words, "Tidal wave coming!" I was sitting in the study facing north, and I had the sense that it was coming from my left, or from the west.

"LORD, I ask you to speak into this," I said.

"Greg, this is a spiritual wave that is about to land on the shores of your country. Yes, expect it to roll across from west to east, and when it has run its course, it will reverse itself and roll over the entire country in the other direction, and from sea to sea to sea. No place will be left out of its reach and no place will be without excuse to what has really transpired over Canada. For I am rolling out My holy presence upon the shores of your nation like never before, and unlike I ever will again. This is the wave

I showed you almost twenty years ago and it *will* bring the renewal that I spoke about in that visitation.

"My Church in Canada will have no capacity to manage this on her own; but that is a good thing! For as you turn to Me and call out to Me for direction, guidance and resources, *you will find Me!* I will show you what I have planted in you all along, and this will grow up so naturally—so vibrantly—you will be astounded at how easy it is to minister in this way and why you could not find this rhythm before.

"The waves will wash away the preconceived ways and notions; the tracks of doing things and methods that really were not working but held traditional value. Instead, you will find new tracks to run on and new rhythms that are perfectly in tune with My Spirit that respond to the reality of the New Day that is fast approaching—is here! The wave that moves in one direction will remove what must be removed. The wave that moves opposite of the first will bring the finishing work to all of this so that My Bride becomes all that I have called her to be in this moment! There is a great transformation that is coming and it is about to crash upon your shores!"

> Arise and shine, for your light has come, and the glory of the LORD rises upon you. See, darkness covers the earth and thick darkness is over the peoples, but the LORD rises upon you and His glory appears over you. Nations will come to your light, and kings to the brightness of your dawn. Isaiah 60:1-3 NIV

~THIRTEEN~

God's Glory and the New Day

The LORD of Heaven's Armies says, "The day of judgement is coming, burning like a furnace. On that day the arrogant and the wicked will be burned up like straw. They will be consumed—roots, branches, and all.

"But for you who fear My name, the Sun of Righteousness will rise with healing in His wings. And you will go free, leaping with joy like calves let out to pasture. On the day when I act, you will tread upon the wicked as if they were dust under your feet," says the LORD of Heaven's Armies.

Malachi 4:1-3

Light Overwhelming Darkness June 8/2020

I prayed through my cleansing prayer and then asked Jesus where He wanted me to read. I had a hard time discerning what book of the Bible He was directing me to other than I kept hearing the number "9". I decided to look again for Jesus and could see that He was holding a short piece of pipe or tubing. It was only about a foot in length and approximately the same diameter. He held it so that one of the ends faced me.

"This represents your time in the tunnel," He said.

"But LORD, time is nothing to you, but for us…" I whined to Him.

"Notice that the length of the tube does not allow darkness to move in either direction. In fact, light is overcoming the darkness within from both sides."

"How are we to understand this?" I asked.

Jesus quoted 1 Corinthians 2:9 to me, "No eye has seen, no ear has heard, and no mind has imagined what God has prepared for those who love Him. For it was to us that God revealed these things by His Spirit. For His Spirit searched out everything and shows us God's deep secrets." But then Jesus added this, "As quickly as I allowed the Covid-19 virus to come on the scene, I will take it away!"

The Mysterious Disc July 23/2020

I asked the LORD where He wanted to meet, and as usual, I found Him sitting in His chair. I sensed that He was holding some sort of large disc or round thing on His lap.

"Stay with this, Greg, and you will see it," He coached. It seemed to be more of a disc than a ball and He held it upright, on edge.

"What is it?" I asked.

"Greg, you will get the opportunity 'discover' what this disc is soon. It will be beneficial to you, your family and the church. Know that I have a perfect plan laid out ahead for you all."

The next day, Jesus brought us right back to the subject of the disc.

"Don't you want to know more about the disc?" He asked, clearly more excited than I was.

I sat there thinking that I now thought of it more as a wheel than a disc.

"And what do wheels do?" Jesus asked perceptively.

I answered, "They roll." I then heard the term 'Wheel of Revival' in my spirit. I knew that there was much weight in the wheel, though in Jesus' hands it appeared weightless. Another picture would be like a stone that would be rolled away from a tomb.

The Mysterious Disc Again July 26/2020

"Let's talk about Iona, Scotland," the LORD began. "You have forgotten that the place where you spent time with Me that day on the island was called Martyr's Bay."

"Why is this significant?"

"You are (and have been) chasing revival for some time. True revival always brings worldly opposition. In this case, the violent and immoral Viking raiders killed 68 monks who were determined to light revival fires all over Great Britain. They stood strong in their faith right up to the end. Greg, these are the embers you brought back with you!"

As I looked at Jesus, I could see the disc/wheel on His lap again. It looked more like a wheel made of stone now than it did before. As I watched it, the stone began to rotate and I sensed that it was gaining speed. The LORD was no longer holding it, yet it stayed vertical above His knees suspended in the air.

"Greg, this wheel is not only gaining momentum, it is gaining weight as well."

Immediately, I thought of the word 'traction'.

"Yes, that is precisely what is happening in this season, He stated. "My glory—My presence manifested on the earth—is finding traction throughout the world, but especially in Western Canada. I will use you (and the friend that had travelled to Iona with me) to spread the embers of My martyrs who toiled for true revival and stood in reverent fear of Me, rather than fearing man. You have the picture of Iona Abbey and the Grass Market monument to the persecuted Covenanters on your screensaver to remind you of this, despite really realizing it.

"You must seek to be fully grounded in Me and My Word moving forward. It is the only way to act with boldness on My behalf. There is more here than just digging up old wells. I am offering a fresh spring in this season, and everyone who comes and tastes of this living water will be changed! I, the Living God, decree it!"

The Coming 24/7 Church August 11/2020

"Where are you this morning, Jesus? What's on Your mind?"

"There's a new theme I want to talk about. You've heard Me say that where My glory rests, that place will never close. It will be open for My people continually (and anyone seeking Me). You (and others you will share this with) find this hard to understand.

"Yes, Greg, once you experience this personally, it will make it easier for you to grasp why both those inside and outside the Church do not want to leave it. I tell you that just like the revivals that have sprung up in history, those who have discovered these well-springs will tell others, while there will be some who are simply drawn to this source of true life.

"Like concentrations of warm water in a lake, these pods of My glory will be interspersed throughout your region. They will hold on to certain aspects of their own expression of My church but all will align with the aspects that I am bringing to this New Day.

"Greg, this isn't about staffing—it's about gifting! Where My presence is there are ample resources provided to accommodate any needs that arise. My Bride will operate in the gifts and talents that I have given her. There will not only be a willingness for all to serve in their natural giftings, but an increased desire to do so as well. People will have to be told to go home simply because they will not want to leave! Just think of the gifts that I have given the Body—prophecy, teaching, evangelism, service—just to name a few. As a willingness to operate in these giftings increases, a natural rhythm occurs. You (and the others you lead with) should not be afraid of this happening as this is how My church was designed to operate."

"Jesus, how do we get ready for this?" I asked.

"How do you get ready for a swim? You put on your swimwear and slide in. It will be as simple as that. Here is My main point: *Wherever My glory exists there will be 24/7 worship and ministry taking place, but it will occur naturally and be supernaturally sustained.* It is all part of the wondrous days ahead!"

An Acceleration Coming September 18/2020

"Greg, I am the God who never sleeps. I am available to you always. This is how the disciples learned to function in the early days of My Church being formed."

"I must always be the source of your power and your focus. Apart from Me you can do nothing substantial or lasting. This season is highlighting the choice: Struggle on your own, or look for Me. The time has already arrived. My Bride is being purified and perfected in these days, though few see it now. Again, this will change as the days go by. You are now in the Malachi 4 days and I am bringing My Bride much joy! Be patient and follow Me into this.

"I am now accelerating things in the physical that have lagged behind the spiritual. Progress on your church building project will speed up because I will it to be so. This will match the great awakening that is coming. My people will naturally awaken to this New Day as they re-engage together as My Church.

"You are right to discern that you are a 'rescue city', a city of refuge. I have given your city and your church site in particular all of the resources necessary to minister to your community in great power and authority. These can only be accessed by cultivating a deep and intimate relationship with Me by embracing the ways of My Spirit.

"It is My presence, manifested in greater glory, that will be both attractive and repelling in the days ahead. Those who are broken hearted, beat down and in great need will come in humility and want; they will not be turned away and will find great healing. But those who inwardly mock Me and hold onto pride will find it very difficult to be around My Bride.

"Greg, this is manifesting right now in places all around the world. As this 'pops up' in your circles, it will be disorienting at first (My attractive presence) as it is different and more powerful than you, or anyone around you, have ever experienced or witnessed. Just embrace what you see happening in your midst; trust Me as this unfolds. For this is the gateway to the Malachi 4 season ahead. Yes, Greg, trust Me!

> The LORD of Heaven's Armies says, "The day of judgment is coming, burning like a furnace. On that day the arrogant and the wicked will be burned up like straw. They will be consumed—roots, branches, and all.
> "But for you who fear my name, the Sun of Righteousness will rise with healing in his wings. And you will go free, leaping with joy like calves let out to pasture. On the day when I act, you will tread upon the wicked as if they were dust under your feet," says the LORD of Heaven's Armies." Malachi 4:1-3

Declare the New Day September 23/2020

"Why has it taken me so long to come to you this morning?" I asked.

Jesus responded, "You have been under a spirit of witchcraft. It has wanted to 'shut you up' as well as 'shut you down'. It came through family lines between 2 and 3 a.m. last night and its effects have lingered since."

"How do we manage this moving forward?" I inquired.

"Greg, how do you mange anything moving forward? You keep your eyes on Me! Everything else is shifting sand, but you build on the solid rock when you come to Me and believe."

"What do I need to know about my zoom meeting tonight?"

"Don't be disturbed at the disorientation that is taking place. Remember, things had to move into this state to remove the bad as well as receive the good. This will only go on for a short time longer. In the meantime, hold your ground. Refuse to compromise. Declare the New Day, for it is here! Prepare for the harvest, as there is great joy on the way! Pray for others and do not judge. Wait for My movement to begin, for it is surely coming!"

Pandemic Over? September 24/2020

"Well, what's on your heart today, LORD?" I began.

"Let's talk about the gap between when the world is saying the pandemic will be over, and *when I say* it will be over. What have I said about evil spirits ruling the day?"

"They are deceptive, lying and controlling spirits," I responded.

"And who is directing all of this?" He asked.

"Satan, his hierarchy of powers and principalities, and willing, but deceived, human participants."

Jesus continued His questioning. "So, if the world is telling you that this pandemic is going to go on for the next couple of years, should you believe it?"

"No. but there is such pressure to lead responsibly and plan, that there doesn't seem to be any alternative," I mused.

"Unless…"

"Unless we (the Church) *really* start to believe that you God, are going to step in."

"And what have I been telling you and all of My prophetic voices (who are truly listening) that I am going to do?" Jesus continued to push.

"You have said that you are coming in glory and this change will come upon us suddenly/quickly."

"And what am I waiting for?"

"Your Church to align with You," I replied quickly.

"And what does this start with?"

"Our true declaration of your sovereignty and power over *all* things. To declare that you are coming to your Church in this New Day; that it will be like the last chapter of Malachi," I answered.

"So, what can I do with the faith of a few?"

"You turned the world right-side up with a few followers 2,000 years ago."

"That's right, and I can do it again!" Jesus said with animation. "I am asking you to stand firm! Trust what I have said, am saying, and will speak to in the days ahead. You were made for this season and I will provide for you as long as you stay in step with Me. Wait on My timing and obey My nudges to speak. Watch and see how things begin to turn toward the truth. You are not going to have to wait too long. Stand your ground!"

Saul to Paul October 21/2020

> Then the Church throughout Judea, Galilee and Samaria enjoyed a time of peace and was strengthened. Living in the fear of the Lord and encouraged by the Holy Spirit, it increased in numbers. Acts 9:31

"LORD, what's on your heart?"

"Greg, what happened to Saul in this chapter?"

I responded, "You met Him on the road to Damascus and he was struck blind."

"Why do you think that I chose to do this?"

"Saul's perspective was all wrong. He was seeing things and acting 180 degrees from how You saw them, and how You wanted things to go," I mused.

"So why blindness?" Jesus prompted.

"It seems that blindness was the only way to get his full attention. Like turning the lights off at a party, it interrupts conversation and immediately draws attention."

"Yes, but what did Paul say he saw that stopped him on the road?"

I answered, "A great light."

"So then, what does blindness have to do with seeing the light?" Jesus continued His quizzing.

"Compared to Your presence and the truth of who you are, what Paul was seeing and how he was understanding You was completely shaded with darkness. I'm not sure how I would be able to handle three days of lost sight, not knowing if I was ever going to see again."

"I sent Ananias to Paul to reverse the blindness as I needed someone to impart the fear of the Lord and one who had enough faith to speak forth *true sight* into someone who had previously stood so against My followers. Ananias feared Me more than Saul's callous reputation and the authority he carried in persecution.

"There is a great light coming to many like this, Greg. There will be many turn-arounds like this, as I upset the strongholds of Satan in the culture around you. You will see some removed from their office or place of authority. Others will simply have a Saul-Paul conversion, where one day they are indifferent to Me, the next, sold-out witnesses of My power and presence. Even now, this seems incomprehensible to you, but so did Paul's conversion in his day, and look what it did! If there is to be a mighty awakening and the change that I have predestined to take place, this must be so. Watch and see!"

My Church is Rising October 23/2020

"LORD, I push out any doubt or unbelief, and I trust in what You have said to me as truth," I said to Him, shaking off unbelief in the process.

"Greg, why does Satan use deception as his main weapon?" He asked in return.

"It seems that it is the only way to turn us from the path of absolute truth. Deception leads us into thinking that *we* know the truth, when in actuality we are following lying suggestions."

"So, why does anything that has to do with an election bother you so much?"

"I guess that it is because there are so many lies that are declared as truth, often from both sides," I responded.

"And how do you think that I feel about this?" Jesus queried. "There is a sweeping movement of My truth coming, for as I draw near, so does truth for that is My very essence. Apart from Me there is no truth. Those who deny Me cannot walk in truth, as there is no truth in what they say because all they have stated and acted upon omits Me and My ways. This includes My lordship over all. There is no real division that matters other than those who choose to follow Me and those who do not. That is why you heard Me speak to the wheat and the tares earlier in the year.

"We are fast approaching—it is actually here—the time of reckoning. The exposure of wickedness and sin that is coming is part of My mercy upon the people of the earth. As I pull away every covering that has hidden the most wicked of enterprises, the opportunity to repent and acknowledge the truth as it relates to Me will be there for all—inside and outside of My Church. 'Judgement comes upon the house of the Lord first…' and from this will come a holy reversal and awe that will spill out into all sides of culture, from what transpires in the Body.

"Can't you see it?" Jesus exhorted. "My Church is about to rise in greater splendor and power than it has ever been in all of history! Look to the east and look to the west; the fields are ripe for the harvest! Look to the north and look to the south; My angels are ready to do everything I have called them to!

"Do not lose faith and don't lose heart. The deceptive debris that swirls and blinds and chokes will last only a short time longer. Even the U.S. president is declaring this in his own way, and as My Church begins to declare this, so will the chaos and confusion end. You will soon see My sovereignty at work and this will overwhelm many. Stand firm in My Word and My promises to you. Do not be deceived!"

When Covid-19 is Removed November 2/2020

"LORD, why is there so much 'push back' against the idea that You can remove the virus suddenly/quickly?" I began.

"Greg, I have spoken of the immense power of the storm of lies over you right now. Like the gold mining divers that you watch in Alaska on TV, the 'vis' or visibility to see Me and My truth requires very close proximity to Me in this moment. Many think that they are close to Me when they really are not. If what the world is telling you lands with more of a punch than what I am saying in the quiet of the day, then that should be evidence enough.

"This is why when I pull the virus away and it dissipates, many will continue to act and believe that it is still around. The hidden agenda of those who have promoted this will require them to keep up the appearance of the pandemic for as long as possible, to try to achieve their desired goals and what they were trying to accomplish through all of this.

"But My Church must be able to see through this and begin to walk in the New Day of My glory, which will be seen in greater and greater measure. It will start with My remnant and quickly gain traction as the reality of this (My glory) takes hold. Yes, much of this coincides with you meeting together in-person again, as you will 'shoot forward' by believing the truth of what I have done and the synergy of My Body brought together again. The unspeakable joy that will come from all of this will be undeniably and irresistibly real to all who pass by.

"This is all part of the Great Awakening coming to the world.

> For as the waters fill the sea,
> the earth will be filled with an awareness
> of the glory of the LORD. Habakkuk 2:14

"Suddenly/quickly, people's eyes will open to the reality of My existence and presence. There will be a holy awe of Me as all who desire to believe what they are experiencing will understand some of the depth of My holiness, splendor and sovereignty. This will be eye-opening for both those who have followed Me for some time, as well as new believers. And this will cause even greater division in the world, as those who reject Me become agitated and push further into rebellion.

"But for those who accept Me and choose to follow My ways, they will walk in the benefits and power of the Sun of Righteousness and My Church will grow in power and strength!"

Does God Not Have the Strength? November 19/2020

Last night after a rather difficult meeting, I woke up at 3:56 a.m. I could feel the gentle nudge to get up and pray, though I could have easily rolled over and gone back to sleep. Instead, I got up and went quietly into the walk-in closet to pray, as I had been doing. As I prayed in the

Spirit, one particular phrase continued to be repeated again and again.

Finally, after about 15 minutes, the LORD's voice came to me in English, revealing what I was saying in another language: "And My people say, 'Does God not have the strength…'" In the physical I laughed out loud reflexively. Then I heard, "He surely does!" as if speaking that God doesn't have the power to end the pandemic is the funniest thing spoken of in heaven.

Jesus was rather stern when He began to speak. "This is the beachhead of the coming movement, Greg. There must be enough of My remnant standing on the truth that *it is I* that will end the incarceration of My people.

"You must have compassion upon My Church as they are disoriented and confused. Most leaders are grappling for any sort of solid direction, as you would, given the circumstances. I have said that I have already enacted and decreed the end of the virus and this is true. But remember who most are listening to: the lying and deceptive spirits working through the media and other sources. I tell you that they will do everything in their power to make false reports and extend the negative effects of the lockdowns and protocols.

"Greg, it is My Church that holds the keys to unlocking and exposing this faster. You can do nothing on your own to expedite this, and this is where deception has crept in. No, My Church must draw into Me and listen to Me only. Then My plans and what I am actually doing in this hour will become abundantly clear to anyone willing to listen!

"Do not take on this burden for it is way too heavy to lift in your own power! I have simply called you (along with others that I have called) to walk in step with Me and do what I call you to do. Our short nightly meetings have done more to attack the enemy strongholds than you can dream or imagine. Know that I am with you in this. Be patient! You will see things turn around very soon!"

Embers of Renewal November 25/2020

Last night as I was watching TV, the LORD's voice broke in saying, "Let's go to war!" I knew that He was inviting me to join Him in the night to pray. Sure enough, Jesus invited me into our closet to pray just before 3:00 a.m. I was careful to follow Him into what He wanted to pray about by praying in the Spirit, but I could tell that much of it was about reclaiming what the enemy had stolen from me recently. These middle-of-the-night sessions continue to grow in strength and duration.

"Jesus, what would be important for me to know today? What is on your heart?" I asked when I met with Him in my usual quiet time.

"Greg, you heard it said on a podcast that it was the second lockdown in Melbourne, Australia, that turned a majority of people to think about spiritual things. The same thing is about to happen here, though to a lesser degree. Regardless, I am setting the tinder for a great fire of restoration!

"You are sensing that many people around you are at a breaking point, mostly because the blanket-like covering of despair and hopelessness the enemy has placed over you has taken its toll. But you and all the others that I have hidden throughout the whole earth have nurtured and taken care of the restorative embers of My glory, and these are about to be fanned into flame by My Spirit! At just the right time I will bring forth the union of My embers and My tinder. When the tinder is fully ignited, it will be introduced to the kindling which, when joined to the stockpiled limbs of My Church, will be an unstoppable bonfire!

"James spoke about the power of the tongue to do great damage. Well, the tongue can be used to do the same, but in reverse. A great movement can be started with the smallest of sparks. And I say to you, you have been carrying this ember for some time!

"'Be holy for I am holy.' This is why you needed to sit on the rocks at Oban and cleanse yourself before travelling on to Iona. And this is why you have had to sit in sabbatical for these past months—time to be introspective, repentant and to seek purity. This is why My Church and the culture she serves must also be paused. This disruptive season is necessary—yes, to reveal the growing evil around you—but more importantly, to transition My Bride to support the holy weight of My glory and the foundation of the heavenly government that is about to be installed *everywhere* (yes, underline that!). For the sake of the great middle mass of people who do not know Me and My true amazing grace, I am doing this."

> The Lord isn't really being slow about His promise, as some people think. No, He is being patient for your sake. He does not want anyone to be destroyed, but wants everyone to repent. 2 Peter 3:9

"This is where things are heading, Greg, and the gates of hell cannot stop this. In fact, the gates of hell are about to fall all over the place, as you will be My witness! This too, is part of the evidence that a New Day has arrived—among many other things!

"Continue to make yourself available to Me when I call as there are important moments to expedite time and move the agenda ahead a great deal. Greg, My Church holds the keys to this and as I awaken her, you will see My love for her in full blossom! Shalom!"

The Reach of The LORD's Sword December 15/2020

"Greg, have I shown you My sword before?" Jesus began. "Yes, I have, and it has always come in the context of freedom and judgement. The two must go hand in hand. I have chosen to speak to you out of My Word so that your faith would be bolstered in all that I am doing in the world (and this includes your city and province). There is no place that My sword is not reaching in this moment—no place! My enemies—those who have been deceived and manipulated by the dragon—have surpassed the time of repentance. They have chosen their fate by remaining either stiff-necked in defiance and belief in their ruse, or they have run to the hills (places of hiding) to escape judgement. This is impossible, as I see where every one of them has scattered to.

"This is not the end of 'the Monster of the Sea' but he will be badly injured and will have little effect on the earth for years to come. This is what I meant when I would tell you that I was dismantling powers and principalities. I have crushed his heads and have retrieved all that is legally mine.

"I *choose* to move now against the narrative—the web of lies and deception that he and his co-conspirators have laid out to the world. The Christmas miracle will once again be seen as I overturn and reverse all that the demonic realm has painted as 'reality'. I am about to reveal to the entire world what the true reality of My Kingdom looks like, and it will be unmistakable!

"Watch as Leviathan sinks to the depths of the sea to lick his wounds in terror and fright, while I immediately calm the waters that—just an instant before—were made so turbulent by his power. My omnipotence is unmatched and this will be on display for all to see. Yes, rejoice in the days ahead for I am bringing joy out of the darkness and peace will reign as My light extends around the world. Behold I bring the New Day, Greg! Proclaim it! Tell others! Prepare to see the wonder of it all!"

Pulling the Plug on Deception December 17/2020

In the middle of a long and sustained time of praying, the LORD's voice came through to me. "The atmosphere is changing, Greg." A few seconds later, "Again, I say to you Greg, the atmosphere is changing." I continued to pray in the Spirit, knowing in my soul that there was a great deal of significance to this morning's prayer time.

"I am pulling the plug," I heard Him say, getting a picture of water rushing in a swirl as the plug is removed. "All the lies and deception that have been over you for so long are being drawn down to the depths of the earth, where they originated. As the delusion recedes, you will see with greater clarity all the machinations and structures that held this evil in place for so long. This is part of the Christmas miracle that I spoke about earlier.

"You are seeing this as a watchman, so don't expect others to understand all of this quite yet, but it won't be long before you feel a part of a company, rather than a lone ranger. You are right to discern that the virus and the deceit go hand in hand. One feeds off the other and it is not your place to understand how this works, but only to know there is a correlation. So, as I drain the deception and all of the concentrated lies with it, so too, I remove the grounds that the virus has to live off of. *That* is why it is disappearing.

"This will be unexplainable to everyone. Your health officials and government will remain on the same tracks as they have been on, believing that it is the actions (protocols) taken that are doing this. Not so! The false narrative of lies is so strong that it will take men and women of great courage to begin speaking the truth of what is really taking place. This is where the groundswell of faith comes into play. What did you read this morning?

> The LORD protects those of childlike faith;
> I was facing death, and He saved Me. Psalm 116:6

"As faith arises, it will bring with it a place for My presence to dwell. This will, in turn, usher in the New Day. Greg, pray that you would have the courage and boldness to speak and do what I have called you to do. Pray for others with similar assignments, as there are many around you like this. They must arise, just as My angelic army has obediently and quickly followed My call to action.

"Take courage! Remain strong! The battle is Mine, says the LORD! There is no lens for you to use in understanding fully all that I am about to bring upon the earth. But rejoice! You are going to marvel at all that I am bringing forth! Yes, Greg. Wait, watch and wonder!"

Jesus and His Lists December 23/2020

After reading through Joshua 1-3, Exodus 15 and Job 1 and 2, I looked for Jesus. I could see Him comfortably resting across from me holding a modern pen and a coil notepad that flipped pages over the top vertically. "Why are you showing me this notepad, LORD?" I asked.

"Greg, I'm here to encourage you," He replied. "It is not easy to stay focused on Me and who I am in the midst of the Great Storm. I am listing all of the ways you have stuck with it—remained in a strong state of relationship with Me so that I can prepare you for what is ahead. I know the unique gifting and shape that you have—I put it there—but I also know how difficult it is to share some of these burdens with others.

"Soon, however, your task *will be* to share with others, and you will need all of the boldness, courage and faith that I have been building in you since before you completed your teaching career. But as the waters begin to recede and you feel the momentum shifting, I will infuse into My followers a supernatural strength as your faith builds. Many of My believers are beginning to understand that the only way out from under such great oppression is a mighty miracle from Me. Giants own the land right now, empowered by supernatural forces. But even these all were made by Me and must submit to My sovereignty when I act. And act I shall! There is a full-on rebellion taking place and the Lord of Hosts is being mocked!

"I have made lists of many things as nothing gets by Me; nothing can remain in the shadows without Me noticing it. Just like the Christmas lists that so many people have made, I have made lists and they are thorough and comprehensive. When I act, it will be like a Red Sea moment! All the nations of the world will know that there is only one God, and there will not be one person who does not see My power for what it is! Who else can make the mighty powers ruling the earth shake with fear? Who else can strangle the strongholds that have moved against My people with such force? Only the Sovereign God of the Universe! Only I have the power to make the Red Sea and Jordan River moments!"

> He (God) did this so all the nations of the earth might know that the LORD's hand is powerful, and so you might fear the LORD your God forever. Joshua 4:24

"This reversal from the fear caused by the virus and the story being told regarding it, to the holy awe of the LORD, will be greatly disorienting. Many will want to believe in the narrative that they have been told over these past months, but I will call forward those who can bear My presence to stand in the Jordan and allow Me to create a way forward for My people. I want to bring them clarity and vision in this day; to shake off the fog made up of manipulation, intimidation and control that has come over them from such overt amounts of witchcraft and satanism. You aren't necessarily one of these, but you are to encourage leaders to stand and uphold My presence so that the ugly waters of the storm can be parted. My people *will be* allowed to cross into the New Day! When My people crossed the Jordan, it was the season of harvest, just as it is now. In the natural, it seemed impossible to cross given the river was in flood, just as it seemed impossible to escape Pharaoh and his mighty army. But I tell you I have a way forward from this, and what seems like an impossibility, is in fact, about to happen!

"Greg, I see all that you have done to draw into Me. It is impossible for Me not to notice! Walk out these remaining days of waiting like you have victory, because you do! Hold on to the promises I have given you, for they will not be taken away from you! Encourage others, remain steadfast and in My Word. For you all are about to rejoice like you never have before! Wait, watch and wonder!"

A Celebration is Coming! Jan. 1/2021

I spent some time reading through some gospel readings, when I decided to look up. Jesus sat across from me as usual and the first thing I noticed was that He was wearing a party hat on His head. I found this strange, so I checked the spirit showing me this. After a brief bit of warfare prayer, my vision became even clearer and not only could I see the hat again, but Jesus was also blowing a party favor in my direction. I found this ironic after spending a New Year's Eve on "stay at home" orders.

"Jesus, what is this about?" I inquired.

"Greg, a time to celebrate is just around the corner," Jesus said. "All that you have had stolen from you—personal interaction, public gatherings and the freedom to celebrate holidays and festivals—all of this is about to be returned to you and more!

"You can see Me and what I am portraying because you have learned to look through the eyes of faith! Carnal eyes—eyes that only look at what the world is saying is real—will not reveal what I am revealing to you. In fact, the world system does everything it can to mask Kingdom truth and eliminate any hope in Me from breaking forth.

"But I tell you there is a great celebration ahead! In just a little while you will see things break forth in the natural that are going to overwhelm and overrun the current systems of the world in a positive way. This has already taken place in the Spirit and all of heaven rejoices. And soon the things that you have longed for and hoped that you would see in your lifetime, will burst forth with such color and conviction that you will hardly be able to believe all that you see, hear and experience! My Kingdom is coming and your region is about to be a frontrunner in this!

"The party has started in the heavenly places and this should encourage you to share this with others! It is only by faith that this can gain traction, but find traction it will! I guarantee it! The juxtaposition from the darkness that overcame you in 2020 will be starkly contrasted by the light of My coming glory in 2021. This will cause even the most dedicated skeptic to sit up and take notice of all that is transpiring. Like I have told you before, it will take great effort to refute that it is I Am who created this magnificent turnaround.

"Yes, Greg. Get ready to celebrate! Continue to pray as you have been and encourage others to come to Me wholeheartedly. A great movement is afoot that cannot be stopped—nor would you want it to be! Wait, watch and wonder!"

It's in the Waiting January 27/2021

"LORD, I don't want to set the agenda. I believe that you know exactly what I should know and when I should understand it," I stated.

"Greg, I am thankful that you have that heart stance. There is much that I can do with a surrendered and contrite heart. You are hearing the song lyrics, 'It's in the waiting…' because it has been the waiting on Me that has developed that soft heart. You have no idea how profoundly the Church will change as I call her forth. The transformation will be monumental! This will not happen all at once, however, as there must be a willing, heartfelt desire to leave behind certain parts of the old, so that the new has room to blossom and spring forth. Some expressions of My Body will never get there, but most will revive to My calling and respond to the direct orchestration of My Spirit.

"Of course, there will be frontrunners and you will demonstrate to many others how to receive this wave that I am offering in all of its fullness—how the entire community around you will thrive with vibrant life and activity. I will open the eyes of My people to ways, structures and resources hidden to generations past, but embraced and accepted by this present one. So great are the wonders ahead for you, that you will hardly be able to contain yourselves. You will barely recover from one glorious event, before you experience another episode of My power and holiness. There are the glory days ahead, and everyone will know that there is an authentic move of God afoot!"

The Time Promised by God Has Come February 4/2021

Today's verse:

> "The time promised by God has come at last!" He announced. "The Kingdom of God is near! Repent of your sins and believe the Good News!" Mark 1:15

"LORD, what's on Your heart for today?" I asked.

"Well, Greg, what is the first line of the verse above?"

"*The time promised by God has come at last!*" I answered.

"This is a pretty obvious statement, is it not?" Jesus stated. "I feel the anxiety rising up in you again, even after you read through your entire manuscript once more yesterday. What I have said to you, I have said to few others, in terms of specific events. You received both the timeline and the privilege of turning pages in the *Book of Things to Come.* So why the trepidation now? What was the second thing that I said in today's verse?"

"*The Kingdom of God is near!*" I specified.

"This occurred as I started My ministry on earth and declared the 'then' New Day—and it certainly was one! But that statement was meant to be used more than once. Yes, it was for this very moment as well. The Kingdom of God is not only near—it approaches in great fullness! No other force in all of the cosmos can do what My Kingdom is about to do throughout the entire world. The housecleaning that you are about to witness will be beyond your comprehension and will affect the earth for generations to come! You can feel it coming now if you really try to. Don't let the dreariness of the cold days of winter fool you—spring is right around the corner and so is great joy and celebration!

Jesus continued, "The third part of this statement is: *'Repent of your sins and believe the Good News!'* My Kingdom can only truly be accessed by those who have chosen a route of repentance. Otherwise, they are blind and deaf to its reality, even though it will surround them! The other key piece is belief. It is not enough to just repent and turn from your wicked ways. No, it must be followed by an authentic belief in My existence, My character, and My presence among you. *This* is what I dwell in and I inhabit the praises of My people. Faith, trust, belief, hope and expectation—these are all the elements that allow Me to freely move and the foundation that My Kingdom rests on. This is all coming your way, because this is building among an ever-growing remnant of My true followers!

"My Kingdom approaches—is actually here—and as it is realized by more of My followers, you will see the changes I spoke about in your book. Do not be shaken and do not lose your faith. For I come suddenly/quickly to gain back everything that was lost and to bring restoration to a dry and needy land. It is time to celebrate and rejoice! Shalom!"

Afterword

If you have made it this far, chances are you have realized that there are some parts of what I was hearing that were somewhat off, need a great deal of interpretation, or their essence still needs to be revealed. On this side of eternity, we only see in part; we simply catch bits and pieces of the ebb and flow in the voice of the King.

Yet prophesy in its purest form is not foretelling as much as it is *forthtelling*. True words that come to us from the LORD always derive from His heart and are intended to encourage and uplift. We must test what we hear and to trust what we've heard as it must line up with Scripture.

Paul wished that we all would learn to pray in the Spirit, but preferred that we would also learn to prophesy instead.

> I wish you could all speak in tongues, but even more I wish you could all prophesy. For prophecy is greater than speaking in tongues, unless someone interprets what you are saying so that the whole church will be strengthened. 1 Corinthians 14:5

Praying in the Spirit can sometimes alienate or confuse those in the Body of Christ who don't fully understand it, and have yet to experience its power and revelatory qualities. Rather than this, Paul—speaking of prophecy—pointed to the impact of speaking to others under the *inspiration* of the Holy Spirit.

Over this last season, prophecy has been under attack not because it was encouraging (and for the most part, it was) but because it was looked to as a method of predicting future happenings and events. Since many of the forecasts did not come to fruition in *timely manner* or in ways that we *expected them*, many threw up their hands in frustration, rather than pushing through *with faith* to hang on to the Word of God and the promises that He was speaking over His Church.

A large reason for recording My visits with the LORD in book form have to do with bringing clarity and direction to a very disoriented and hurting world. In many ways, this also includes Jesus' Church. We have just endured a very turbulent, undependable and chaotic season. Little in the world seemed trustworthy or honest. The storm appeared to have no end in sight. Yet, Jesus...

The hope of the Christian Church has been, is, and always will be found in the saving grace of our Lord Jesus Christ! By His sacrificial death on the cross 2,000 years ago, He won the battle over sin and death which hangs over every person that has walked the earth. This victory has been secured for all time, and when we humble ourselves and admit that we need saving, He stands before us with arms wide-open.

> The sacrifice that You (God) desire is a broken spirit. You will not reject a broken and repentant heart, O God. Psalm 51:17

If you have not accepted Jesus as your Lord and Savior, I invite you to do this now. And if you have already done this, I encourage you to grow the two-way relationship with Jesus that is available now, simply by spending time in His Word and with Him. Find a quiet place, at a regular time and pull up an empty chair just for the LORD. Allow our loving, living God to open your eyes and ears to His reality, truth and wisdom.

Yes, Almighty God is the same yesterday, today and forever. His love never fails and His mercy endures forever. Try Him at His word!

About the Author

Greg Gibson has been attending St. Albert Alliance Church for more than 25 years and has acted in various capacities as a lay leader. He operates in the spiritual gifts of *prophecy* and *teaching*.

Greg is also a *watchman*, the actual meaning of his given first name. As a *watchman*, he often sees things coming before most of the Church body does, much like a lookout posted high on a rampart would see into the distance.

Finally, Greg is a *gatekeeper* as well. Biblical gatekeepers were not only charged with overseeing the gates to the city or temple, but were also responsible for protecting the resources and cleansing the temple.

Combined, these giftings have uniquely shaped his calling and ministry.

To contact Greg, please email him at
Forefrontcanada@gmail.com

Looking for Jesus

PRAYER

Seeking the Intimacy of God's Presence

Gregory A. Gibson

When communicating with others,
few of us would think of holding our hands over our ears or closing our eyes. Yet until now, this basically describes what our times of prayer have been like.

Jesus is calling us to look for Him!

Looking for Jesus Prayer *explains what this prayer is,* explores the reasons why Jesus is calling His followers to look for Him by the power of the Holy Spirit and by doing so, how to enjoy the intimacy of God's presence in personal and corporate prayer.

This type of prayer is strategic and crucial if the Church is to be all it is meant to be.

"But we do know that we will be like Him, for we will see Him as He really is." 1 John 3:2

FOREFRONT

CANADA  MINISTRIES

$14.95 CAN

www.ingramcontent.com/pod-product-compliance
Lightning Source LLC
Chambersburg PA
CBHW051950090426
42741CB00008B/1334
* 9 7 8 1 7 7 3 5 4 2 8 4 3 *